FAMOUS FIGHTS OF INDIAN NATIVE REGIMENTS

FAMOUS FIGHTS OF INDIAN NATIVE REGIMENTS

REGINALD HODDER

GYAN

Published by

GYAN

Gyan Publishing House
5, Ansari Road
Daryaganj, New Delhi-110002
Phone: 011-47034999, 9811692060
E-mail: books@gyanbooks.com

Distribution Network
gyanbooks.com
India, USA, Canada, UK, Australia, France

ISBN: 978-81-212-9316-7 (PB)
First Published, 1914

2nd Impression 2023

Printed at: Gyan Press, Delhi.

AMOUS FIGHTS OF INDIAN NATIVE REGIMENTS

Author: REGINALD HODDER

The Daily Telegraph
WAR BOOKS

FAMOUS FIGHTS OF INDIAN NATIVE REGIMENTS

WITH THE EXPEDITIONARY FORCE, 1914.

FAMOUS FIGHTS OF INDIAN NATIVE REGIMENTS

By

REGINALD HODDER

Author of "British Regiments at the Front," &c.

HODDER AND STOUGHTON

LONDON NEW YORK TORONTO

MCMXIV

The Author wishes to express his indebtedness to Mr. J. Norvill for his valuable assistance and suggestions.

THE PADISHA'S WORDS

"I look to all my Indian soldiers to uphold the Izzat of the British Raj against an aggressive and relentless enemy.

"I know with what readiness my brave and loyal Indian soldiers are prepared to fulfil this sacred trust on the field of battle shoulder to shoulder with their comrades from all parts of the Empire. Rest assured that you will always be in my thoughts and prayers.

"I bid you to go forward and add fresh lustre to the glorious achievements and noble traditions of courage and chivalry of my Indian Army, whose honour and fame are in your hands."

CONTENTS

ORDER OF THE DAY.—No. 1.

SOLDIERS OF THE INDIAN ARMY CORPS,

We have all read with pride the gracious message of his Majesty the King-Emperor to his troops from India.

On the eve of going into the field to join our British comrades, who have covered themselves with glory in this great war, it is our firm resolve to prove ourselves worthy of the honour which has been conferred on us as representatives of the Army of India.

In a few days we shall be fighting as has never been our good fortune to fight before, and against enemies who have a long history.

But is their history as long as yours? You are the descendants of men who have been mighty rulers and great warriors for many centuries. You will never forget this. You will recall the glories of your race. Hindu and Mahomedan will be fighting side by side with British soldiers and our gallant French Allies. You will be helping to make history. You will be the first Indian soldiers of the King-Emperor who will have the honour of showing in Europe that the sons of India have lost none of their ancient martial instincts and are worthy of the confidence reposed in them.

In battle you will remember that your religions

enjoin on you that to give your life doing your duty is your highest reward.

The eyes of your co-religionists and your fellow-countrymen are on you. From the Himalayan Mountains, the banks of the Ganges and Indus, and the plains of Hindustan, they are eagerly waiting for the news of how their brethren conduct themselves when they meet the foe. From mosques and temples their prayers are ascending to the God of all, and you will answer their hopes by the proofs of your valour.

You will fight for your King-Emperor and your faith, so that history will record the doings of India's sons and your children will proudly tell of the deeds of their fathers.

JAMES WILLCOCKS,
Lieut.-General
Commg. Indian Army Corps.

CAMP, Oct. 10th, 1914.

INTRODUCTION

Our native army in India is principally composed of Sikhs, Pathans, Punjabi Mussalmans, and Gurkhas. Each of these races has acquired in its own way a high reputation for valour and martial skill, and it need not be doubted that the men drawn from these sources in the East to confront a relentless foe in the West are absolutely reliable.

Quite a third of the Indian Army is composed of Sikhs. They are not exactly a race, but are a military and religious caste, the only modern importation into their religion being a savour of socialism. The Sikh sect dates from the fifteenth century, when Baba Nanak raised them, so to speak, from the indiscriminate mass, to governing positions in the Punjab. This was partly owing to their strong religious sentiment, but principally to their military capabilities. In course of time, they came to dominate the whole of Northern India, and reached the height of their power under the Maharajah Runjit Singh (1780-1839). The Sikh wars of 1845-6 and 1848-9 are a matter of history. In these both British and Sikhs fought with the utmost gallantry. But, since 1849, the brave Sikhs have been loyal British subjects, and have fought on our side not only in the Indian Mutiny, but in Abyssinia, Afghanistan, China, Burma, Somaliland, and Tibet. At the present time, the Indian Army includes thirteen Sikh battalions, and there are one or more Sikh squadrons in each of the cavalry regiments, as well as a company or two in each of the infantry battalions.

The Khalsa Sikh is the beau-ideal of everything high and noble in the Sikh race. Stirred by the depths of his own religion, he fought and conquered at its behest. And to him is owing the high reputation and romantic popularity of an honoured name. The Khalsa Sikh is derived from many different castes, but principally from the Jats of the Punjab, whose character has responded to, and whose development has been moulded by, the self-reliant, warlike, and manly teachings of their ideal lawgiver and hero, Govid

Singh, from whom their name is derived—the word Sikh being originally Singh.

It is to the Jat element that the Sikh owes his most lofty characteristics. Thus the Jat Sikh respects himself wisely. His racial pride is based on the knowledge that he is justly, and without doubt, the flower of India. With him, as with all others who undertake great deeds in the present, the natural stimulus to such deeds is the stirring song of heroic achievements in the past.

The Pathans emanate from the Afghan race, and inhabit the hills of the north-west frontier of India. While many of the clans are Shiahs, the majority are orthodox Mussalmans. These Pathans, who frequently figure in novels dealing with Indian life, are, in their way, romantic figures. They are not only tall, handsome, and striking in appearance, but they have also a very independent character, obeying discipline for discipline's sake, and their officers for love of them. It is very strange that their facial characteristics are decidedly Jewish in type. It may be asked why there are only Company regiments, and no Class regiments of the Pathans. The reason is that, while they do not possess all the qualities which make for the complete efficiency of the Class regiment, they have unusual merits which are a very desirable leaven to almost any body of fighting men. They are certainly an admirable factor in combination with Sikhs and Punjabi Mussalmans.

The Punjabi Mussalmans were the original inhabitants of the Punjab, and their strong characteristics are still uppermost in that province. By race they are both Rajput and Jat, but their clans are many. From their wealthy families are recruited many fine cavalry regiments. They have a particular leaning towards mountain cavalry work, and this tendency has been fostered by the Government. Taking them all round, they are most efficient and courageous soldiers, and their attachment to their officers is proverbial.

As to the Gurkha, he needs but slight introduction. He is, so to speak, the "Little Benjamin" of the force from India, and excites great interest by his high courage and remarkable skill.

Introduction

When the Gurkhas were told that they were wanted to fight in the great war they asked, " Shall we all be killed?"; and the officer said, "Not all." They inquired, " Shall a great many be killed ? " He replied, " Possibly." Then they asked, " Will a hundred come back ? " " Perhaps so." " That will be enough," they said ; " our people will know that we have fought well."

The Gurkha's skill with his *kukri* is so remarkable as to appear absolutely unerring. Given a human mark—let us say in the shape of a German—he can take off his nose or ear, or pierce his eye with deadly precision. No knife-thrower in the world can so accurately and closely fence in a man standing against a wall as can a Gurkha with some twenty knives—without drawing a drop of blood. A soldier writing from the front concludes his mention of these terrible little men with the passage: " God help the Germans these men come across, for nobody else can. Death to them is a pastime." Yet, though the art of throwing the *kukri* is perfection itself among the Gurkhas, it must not be supposed that they make a practice of throwing it at the enemy.

They would not run the risk of losing the beloved weapon for the sake of killing *one* German.

The well-known fighting races inhabiting the Punjab, such as the Sikhs and Pathans, are supplemented by a considerable number of smaller fighting castes. All these are either of Rajput, Jat, or Tartar descent; but, being mostly Mahomedans, they are prone to claim Moghul or Arab origin. Though not very distinct from some of the more unwarlike Punjab castes, they have, at some period of their history, displayed enough valour to acquire the ascendancy over neighbouring districts, and the memory of this has given them that pride of blood and race and that spirit of self-reliance which so largely constitute the martial instinct. The smaller Mahomedan fighting tribes of the Punjab are often grouped together under the generic term "Punjabi Mahomedan."

The most important, from a military point of view, are the *Ghakkars*, who make excellent soldiers. They are fine men, fierce, proud, and high-spirited.

Awans and *Sials*.—These were at first soldiers,

and latterly agriculturists. During the Mutiny the Sial chief remained loyal, and rendered active assistance by raising a small body of cavalry from his tribe for Imperial use.

The Kharrals are also a well-built, hardy tribe, possessing the martial instinct in a high degree. The Bhattis and the Khokars are also among the warriors of India.

[NOTE.—The warriors of India have a score to settle with the Germans. It is a private matter not to be mentioned in the same breath with the whole-hearted loyalty of the Indian troops, but at the same time it will lend a keener edge to every *kukri*, a more formidable point to every lance and bayonet, a more deadly aim to every bullet. What rankles justly in the Indian's breast in this. During the Boxer Insurrection of 1900 the Germans treated the brave Indian troops fighting by their side as if they had been the dirt of the earth. Our noble Indians, whose traditions were clothed in glory long before the Germans knew proper clothing of any kind, have not forgotten this. For fourteen years they, too, have been looking forward to "the day." And now it has come. "For the Padisha and the Right!"—if one could read their thoughts—"and, incidentally, a squaring of accounts!"]

A GENERAL DESCRIPTION OF THE INDIAN ARMY

COMMANDS.—A Command is one of the principal administrative portions into which the Army of India is divided. There are four such Commands—the Punjab, Bengal, Madras, and Bombay. Each Command is presided over by a Lieut.-General, and is further divided into first and second class districts, commanded by Major-Generals and Brigadier-Generals respectively. The principal executive authority is vested in the Commander-in-Chief in India, subject to the control of the Governor-General, who is, by law, the supreme head of the Army.

NATIVE CAVALRY.—A regiment of native cavalry, with the exception of the Guides and the Lancers of the Hyderabad Contingent, consists of four squadrons. The strength varies slightly, but is usually eight British officers, one medical officer, seventeen native officers, and 608 non-commissioned officers and men.

The native cavalry, with the exception of the Body-Guards and the three regiments of Madras Lancers (now the 26th King George's Own Light Infantry, the 27th Light Cavalry and the 28th

Light Cavalry), is organised on what is called the Silladar System, *i.e.*, the horses, saddlery, clothing, equipment and war arms (except carbines and revolvers) are the private property of the regiment, and are provided for by funds to which all ranks pay donations on joining, with monthly subscriptions throughout their entire service. This system is characteristic of their dignity and standing. The original donation, or *assami*, is returned on a man being pensioned or discharged. A baggage mule or pony, and a driver who acts as grass-cutter, are maintained by every pair of fighting men. Two Sowars, mounted on fast-trotting camels, are attached to each squadron for the rapid conveyance of orders over long distances. The native cavalry is armed with sword and carbine. Lancers carry their own special weapon in addition. All corps are trained in the use of the lance, which in some regiments is carried by the front-rank men.

THE RANKS.—The native ranks and their respective duties are as follow :—

Risaldar-Major.—The chief native officer of the regiment. The badge of his rank is a crown worn on each shoulder-strap. He commands a half-squadron, and is the confidential adviser of the Commandant in all matters relating to the native ranks.

Risaldar and Ressaidar.—Half-squadron commanders. The badge of the former is three stars; of the latter, two stars, worn on each shoulder-strap.

Woordie-Major.—Native adjutant. He is generally a Ressaidar.

Kot Dafadār.—The senior non-commissioned officer of the regiment.

Dafadār.—Sergeant.

Solutri.—Veterinary subordinate.

Sowar.—Trooper.

NATIVE ARTILLERY.—A native mountain battery has an establishment of five British officers, three native officers, and 253 non-commissioned officers and men. The armament consists of six 2.5 in. R.M.L. guns, carried on mules.

The only native field batteries now maintained are those of the Hyderabad Contingent. Each battery consists of two British officials, two native officers, and 128 non-commissioned officers and men. The armament consists of two six-pounder S.B. guns and two twelve-pounder howitzers.

NATIVE INFANTRY.—A single battalion of native infantry is organised in four double companies, and has a complement of nearly twenty British officers, one medical officer, sixteen native officers, and eighty non-commissioned officers. The strength of the rank and file varies from 800 in the Punjab and Bengal to 720 in

Madras and Bombay. To facilitate transfers in war time, the infantry, with a few exceptions, is organised into groups of two or three linked battalions, having a common regimental centre. Each battalion has a reserve, varying in strength from 218 to 160 men.

Native ranks and duties are :—

Subadār-Major.—Principal native officer of the battalion and confidential adviser of the Commanding Officer on all matters relating to the native ranks. He also commands a company.

Subadār.—Company commander.

Jemadār.—Subaltern.

Havildār-Major.—Sergeant-major.

Quarter-Master-Havildār.—Quarter-master-sergeant.

Havildār.—Sergeant.

Naick.—Corporal.

Sepoy.—Private.

Recruiting.—For recruiting purposes, India is divided into districts, each in charge of an officer, who recruits only for some particular race. All recruiting parties detached from regiments work under his orders, and all candidates for enlistment are brought to him for approval after undergoing medical examination. The number of applicants for service, especially for the Silladar Cavalry, is often in excess of the number of vacancies available. Recruits must be from sixteen to twenty-five years of age. There is a comparative scale of chest measurement to height, the minimum in each case being 33 in. and 5 feet 6 in. Special standards are allowed for Gurkhas, Dogras, and Mazhbi Sikhs. A native soldier enlists for three years. At the end of that time he may either claim his discharge or prolong his service up to twenty years, when he becomes entitled to a pension. All enlistments are for general service, with liability to serve wherever required.

Racial Composition.—Regiments of native cavalry and battalions of infantry are organised on the class system. They may be composed entirely of one class, when they are called "Class" regiments, or they may be recruited from three or four classes, kept apart in separate companies, when they are styled "Class Company" regiments. For instance, the 14th Sikhs, composed of eight companies of Sikhs, would be an example of the former, while the 30th Punjab Infantry, composed of four companies of Sikhs, two of Dogras, and two of Punjabi Mussalmans, would serve as an example of the latter.

Forage and Rations.—The native soldier pays for his own food and, in the Silladar Cavalry, also for the upkeep of his horse. A regimental bazaar is attached to each corps, from which the men purchase their rations. When the cost of the daily ration exceeds Rs. 3.8.0 per month, compensation is granted by the Government for the difference. On field service the native soldier draws free rations, and in addition to his ordinary pay is granted a special monthly allowance.

QUARTERS.—The quarters of native troops, except in Burma and on the North-west Frontier, are ranges of huts, called lines, which have to be built and kept in order by the corps temporarily occupying them. To defray the cost of repairs, the Government makes an allowance, which is paid monthly.

EDUCATION.—Each regiment and battalion has a school, at which attendance is voluntary. Sepoys are required to pass an easy examination in reading, writing, arithmetic and drill before promoted to non-commissioned rank.

BANDS.—These are maintained by infantry, but not by cavalry. All Gurkha battalions and many corps in which Pathans are enlisted have pipers as well as bandsmen, buglers and drummers. The pipers make their own pipes, in imitation of the Scottish bagpipes, and acquire considerable efficiency under the instruction of Highland band-masters.

FURLOUGH AND LEAVE.—The popularity of service in the native army is largely due to the liberal manner in which furlough and leave are granted.

DRESS.—The dress of the native army is picturesque and distinctive. Kilmarnock caps are worn by the Gurkhas and Garhwalis, otherwise the universal headdress is the turban or pugri. In the Silladar Cavalry all uniforms are provided under regimental arrangements. In the other regiments clothing is issued by the clothing factories at Calcutta and Madras, but the khaki uniform, and all necessaries, such as great-coats, boots, pugris, haversacks, water-bottles, bedding, cooking-pots, etc., are purchased or manufactured regimentally, and may be had from the quartermaster at fixed prices.

Most of our native Indian soldiers are either peasant proprietors or cultivators, and on retirement from service return to their former employment. Some, however, accept minor posts with the civil administration, such as those of caretakers or messengers.

The Indian soldier is generally excellent in sports and athletics. The skill of the Sowar in tent-pegging, lime-cutting, and his daring feats of horsemanship are well known. In the infantry, wrestling is a favourite amusement, and certain classes, more especially Gurkhas, are keen sportsmen in the all-round sense of the word.

Fights of Indian Native Regiments

The military and agricultural classes of India are seen at their best in the native army. Enthusiastic in his profession, endued with great pride of race and considerable spirit, the native soldier feels that there is a *camaraderie* and a community of interests between himself and his British officers which are wholly lacking in his relations with civil officials. Daily intercourse in the lines, and in various games and sports, affords opportunities for mutual acquaintance, and enables British officers to acquire that personal influence over their men which has been so largely responsible for the brilliant results achieved by most of our great men of India.

THE SIKHS

THERE are three great classes of Sikhs: the Sikh by race, the Sikh by religious sect, and the Sikh by political conviction. They are, however, divided tribally as follows:—

The Jat Sikhs,
The Khattri Sikhs,
The Kamboh Sikhs,
The Lobana Sikhs,
The Sikh Chuhras or Mazhbis,
The Sikh Tarkhans,
The Kalal Sikhs.

THE JAT SIKHS.—Our Jat recruits are drawn from the Eastern Jats, a race of hardy husbandmen. They are, so to speak, a clan of Indian agricultural peasantry. They came originally from the highlands of Scythia. These men possess the necessary instincts of the soldier, and their history has been marked by stern, hard fighting.

THE KHATTRI SIKHS.—These are the merchant caste of the Punjabis.

THE KAMBOH SIKHS.—These make excellent soldiers, being of very fine physique and possessing great courage. They have always been noted for their cunning strategy, which now, being far less " slim " than in former times, has developed into the permissible strategy of war.

THE LOBANA SIKHS.—These are the social equals of the Jats.

THE SIKH CHUHRAS or MAZHBIS.—The term " Mazhbis " has now come to be applied to all Chuhras who have adopted Sikhism as their religion. The true Mazhbis are descendants of certain Chuhras, who rescued in a heroic fashion the body of Gurai Teg Bahadur from the Mahomedans, thus saving it from being dishonoured. In return for this, Gurai's son, Govind Singh, bestowed upon them the title of " Mazhbis Rangreeta " (" Chosen Brave "), and invited them into the fold of Sikhism. Therefore the name Mazhbis belongs properly to the descendants of these particular Chuhras' families. Inspired as they are by the glorious history and traditions of Khalsa, these men make excellent soldiers.

SIKH TARKHANS.—Tarkhans are carpenters by caste and profession. They are intelligent and industrious men, of whom about 20 per cent. are Sikhs by religion, the rest being Hindu or Mahomedan. Sikh Tarkhans, if carefully recruited, could supply a fair number of good soldiers.

KALAL SIKHS.—The Kalals are by caste and profession distillers and wine merchants on a small scale. Twenty-five per cent. of these have now embraced Sikhism, the rest being Hindu or Mahomedan; the Hindus being about 50 per cent. of the whole, and the Mahomedans about 25 per cent. Sikh Kalals are often styled Alhuwalias, from the fact that the famous and important Alhuwalia Misb was founded by the Kalal convert to Sikhism. The Chiefs of Kapurthala have always been Kalals by descent, and, since the rise of the Sikh Kalals to political prominence, they have largely given up their original profession to take to the more respectable avocations of merchandise and agriculture. The Kalals have a reputation for "enterprise, mercy and obstinacy"; and the Sikh Kalals make good soldiers, being of good physique and great hardihood.

The stately, manly Sikh has a character all his own. He has the manly virtues of honesty, industry, and tenacity well developed. He is independent, patient, and full of methodical, laborious energy; and, of all the Sikh tribes of whom this description is more or less true, the Jat may be particularly mentioned.

The Sikh race is drawn from the Punjab tribes, such as the Jat and Khattri, who from time immemorial have been renowned for their sturdy grit and independence. It may perhaps be said that the Jat-Sikh combines especially the best qualities of the Pathan races with those of the Sikh tribes.

All the Punjab races are, as a rule, impatient of control, but the Jat is particularly so, exercising in his impatience a fine quality of individual freedom. This, together with the fact that he is neither truculent nor turbulent, provides him with one of the finest qualities of a well-disciplined soldier, in contradistinction to the machine-made soldier. Well understood, he can be, and has been, well managed. Encouraged to continue in his own peaceful agricultural ways, he is reasonable and contented in doing his work; but if he is roused by what he considers unjust aggression, or any unsolicited interference, he is a dangerous man to deal with.

These salient characteristics of the Jat, combined with other qualities cultivated by British rule and example, have tinctured practically the whole Sikh race.

Respect of self and pride of race have now improved from the Sikh character the early intolerance and ungovernable spirit emanating from the Jats. Even the Sikh religion, as taught by its founder Nanak, has modified the hard-and-fast prejudices of the Hindu on the one hand, and on the other has eliminated the baser rancour and fanaticism of the more exoteric Mahomedanism.

The Sikh of to-day is a level-headed, sober-minded, tolerant man, keenly alive to practical issues. And from this may be judged his valour as a soldier. In the thick of battle the Sikh is cool and resolute. He is possessed of grim determination and tenacity. Just as in any emergency of social life he will keep his head with admirable self-restraint, so in the clash of battle he can be relied upon to do the right thing at the right moment in the right way. While not possessing quite so much *élan* as some other tribes, he more than compensates for that lack by his immunity from any tendency to panic.

The high-class Sikh may always be known by his stately bearing and lofty courtesy. His every movement is graceful, and the general impression one would get on the approach of a real Sikh is simply this: "Here comes one who is a prince in his own country." This dignity of bearing extends even to the lower classes, especially among our Sepoys, who carry themselves with an easy elegance, much of which is attributable to their splendid physique and the due consciousness of it.

It is not too much to say that of all the fine races of the East there is no type of man superior to the Sikh. In innate breeding he can tread the razor-edge between independence and insolence, between firm resolution and unreasoning obstinacy, between the present value of tradition and the dead husk of the glorified past. In his respect of himself he commands respect from others, and, combining the essential instinct of the soldier with the acquired love of practical ideals he can see with a single eye what the double-headed vulture of Prussia cannot see with four.

Constant fighting and an iron discipline had kept the Sikhs in order during the lifetime of Ranjit Singh, but after his death the army became unmanageable.

The history of the Sikh War is too well known to need more than passing reference. The troops of the Khalsa were defeated after a series of hard-fought battles, in which they showed soldierly qualities of the highest order. In the decade which followed the conquest of the Punjab, the British Government, impressed with the fighting capacity of their former opponents, determined to employ them as soldiers in their own army.

On the outbreak of the Mutiny, which from the first was identified with the restoration of the Moghul power, there was an immense revival of Sikhism. Hundreds of Sikhs who had turned their swords into ploughshares flocked to Lahore, and eagerly took service in the regiments there being raised by Lord Lawrence. All were filled with an intense longing to range themselves on the side of justice and right. All were anxious to assist in the capture of Delhi—a city associated in their minds with the heroic struggles and reverses of their forefathers. The spirit of the Khalsa, which had suffered greatly by the defeats on the Sutlej, was aroused at the thought of a conflict between Sikhism and Islam—a conflict the memory of which is now not only nobly forgotten, but to be blotted out for ever by heroism and sacrifice; for both Sikh and Mahomedan of India have joined hands in common cause against the enemy of all human progress. Both have espoused our cause with a devotion and loyalty which is almost without parallel in history.

THE SIKH REGIMENTS, WITH THEIR BATTLE HONOURS

Cavalry

The following regiments contain squadrons of Sikhs :—

2nd Lancers (Gardner's Horse).
3rd Skinner's Horse.
4th Cavalry.
6th King Edward's Own Cavalry.
7th Hariana Lancers.
9th Hodson's Horse.
10th Duke of Cambridge's Own Lancers (Hodson's Horse).
11th King Edward's Own Lancers (Probyn's Horse).
12th Cavalry.
13th Duke of Connaught's Lancers.
16th Cavalry.
18th King George's Own Lancers.
19th Lancers (Fane's Horse).

20th Deccan Horse.
21st Prince Albert Victor's Own Cavalry (Frontier Force) (Daly's Horse).
22nd Sam Browne's Cavalry (Frontier Force).
23rd Cavalry (Frontier Force).
25th Cavalry (Frontier Force).
29th Lancers (Deccan Horse).
30th Lancers (Gordon's Horse).
31st Duke of Connaught's Own Lancers.
32nd Lancers.
33rd Queen Victoria's Own Light Cavalry.
36th Jacob's Horse.
37th Lancers (Baluch Horse).
38th King George's Own Central India Horse.
39th King George's Own Central India Horse.

Infantry

The following regiments are composed exclusively of Sikhs :—

14th King George's Own Ferozepore Sikhs.

Raised July 30th, 1846.

Consists of 8 companies of Sikhs.

Badges.—The Plume of the Prince of Wales. The Royal and Imperial Cypher.

Battle Honours.—" Lucknow," " Ali Masjid," " Afghanistan 1878/79," " Defence of Chitral," " China 1900."

Uniform.—*Scarlet,* facings *yellow.*

The Sikhs

15th Ludhiana Sikhs. Raised 1846.

Consists of 8 companies of Sikhs.

Battle Honours.—" China 1860/62," " Ahmad Khel," " Kandahar 1880," " Afghanistan 1878/80," " Suakim 1885," " Tofrek," " Chitral," " Punjab Frontier," " Tirah."

Uniform.—*Scarlet*, facings *emerald green*.

23rd Sikh Pioneers. Raised 1857.

Consists of 8 companies of Mazhbi Sikhs.

Battle Honours. —" Taku Forts," " Pekin," " Abyssinia," " Peiwar Kotal," " Charasiah," " Kabul 1879," " Kandahar 1880," " Afghanistan 1878/80," " Chitral."

Uniform.—*Drab*, facings *chocolate*.

32nd Sikh Pioneers. Raised 1857.

Consists of 8 companies of Mazhbi Sikhs.

Motto.—" *Aut viam inveniam aut faciam.*"

Battle Honours.—" Delhi," " Lucknow," " Afghanistan 1878/80," " Chitral."

Uniform.—*Scarlet*, facings *blue*.

34th Sikh Pioneers. Raised 1887.

Consists of 8 companies of Mazhbi Sikhs.

Battle Honours.—" Chitral," " Punjab Frontier," " China 1900."

Uniform.—*Scarlet*, facings *blue*.

35th Sikhs. Raised 1798, disbanded 1882, re-formed 1887.

Consists of 8 companies of Sikhs.

Battle Honours.—"Punjab Frontier," "Malakand."

Uniform.—*Scarlet*, facings *yellow*.

36th Sikhs. Raised 1858, disbanded 1882, re-formed 1887.

Consists of 8 companies of Sikhs.

Battle Honours. — "Punjab Frontier," "Samara," "Tirah."

Uniform.—*Scarlet*, facings *yellow*.

47th Sikhs. Raised 1901.

Consists of 8 companies of Sikhs.

Uniform.—*Scarlet*, facings *yellow*.

The 48th Pioneers, 51st Sikhs (Frontier Force), 52nd Sikhs (Frontier Force), 53rd Sikhs (Frontier Force), and 54th Sikhs (Frontier Force) are Sikh regiments with other tribes intermixed.

THE RAJPUTS

THE chief characteristic of the Rajput is his pride of blood. Representing as he does the higher military castes of India, his one ambition has always been to wield a sword, and wield it well. For ages in the past the Rajput maintained his supremacy in one or another part of India. Claiming descent from the sun and the moon, and later from those two heroes of the Mahabharata—Rama and Krishna—the Rajput maintains that his ancient and noble blood has flowed in the veins of kings from times more remote than any other history can record. That old but immortal legend of the Bhagavad Gîta, in which Prince Arjuna held a discourse with Krishna, the supreme Deity, in his war-chariot, drawn up between the opposing forces of Kauravas and Pandavas, is regarded by the Rajput as peculiarly his own. It is not to be wondered at, then, that, possessing from time immemorial this lofty poem, so sublime in its aspiration, so pure and tender in its piety, the Rajput has always been a man of high and noble sentiment and lofty ideals. He is, as the literal rendering of his name implies, the " Rajah's son," and in war has always displayed most noble and fearless qualities.

It cannot be said that the Rajput is content to shine in the reflected glory of the past. In ancient times he devoted his life to making epic history, and in these days this serves him for an ever-present tradition from which he will draw the necessary material to add another volume to that history. Let him dream of the past achievements of his race, his ancient glory in war; let him sing the songs that he has made, and shake off the sloth of peace, and so rush into battle; for out of such dreams and stirring songs springs all human greatness.

There is no questioning the bravery and stamina of the Rajput. Under a good commander who knows how to appeal to him, the Rajput will face death in any grim form. He has a spirit so fierce and dauntless that naturally it is tinctured with the changing tides of strong emotion, which at times may have its drawbacks; but he is, even more than the Gurkha, a soldier fit for a special task; indeed, his dash and heroism are so remarkable that even the Gurkha will sometimes claim to be directly descended from the Rajput.

There is no history to record of the Rajput as a race, for each Rajput state and clan—and there are a large number of them—has its own history. Roughly, they may be described as more or less pure-blooded, modern Hindu (Brahminical) representatives of the early Aryan emigrants into India.

> . . . "The mild Hindu
> Of far-off Rajputana,
> (Who) smiles to think how very few
> Will ever reach Nirvana,"

is not the Rajput. It is a mistake to suppose that the Rajputs are the inhabitants of the province bearing their name. They form but a small part of the population of that province, nor are they by any means restricted to it, being found in large numbers from the Indus to Benares. A large section of the Rajputs of the Punjab, having been converted to Mahomedanism, have thereby lost their distinctive character of Rajputs, who, retaining the religion of their forefathers, are essentially Hindu. And among them are seers and philosophers of the highest degree—men whose feet Nietzsche and Treitschke are not worthy to kiss. And in the Rajput's championship of the higher things he is instinct with the wisdom of India, who sends him westward; India, who through the mouth of her sublimest poet says, from a platform undreamed of by the Teutonic philosopher,

> "Near to renunciation—very near—
> Dwelleth eternal peace."

Each separate Rajput clan has its own peculiar customs and rites, while holding the general customs and rites in common with the whole Rajput race. This peculiarity is strongly marked by the fact that the same clan living in different countries has, in addition to its own general clan rights, others which seem to have been born out of its separate environment. The Rajput in Rajputana invariably marries out of his own clan, but if he allows his daughter to marry into a lower clan he suffers in social position. A Rajput may legally marry more than one wife, and he is permitted by his social and moral code certain things which some other codes condemn.

In the process of recruiting among Rajputs it is a simple matter to tell the real from the false by the following points. A true Rajput will eat with his illegitimate children, but not out of the same dish ; he will allow his natural son to smoke his hookah, but only provided he draws the smoke through his closed hand. He will eat food prepared and cooked by the natural children of any Rajput, but he will not eat *with* them, nor under any conditions allow them to smoke his hookah.

The Rajput woman is noted for her bravery and high ideal of honour. Woe betide the husband or brother who has not all his wounds in front. There are many tales of Rajput women snatching a dagger from their waistband and plunging it into their hearts rather than suffer dishonour. There are even stories current as to their fighting ability, telling how on occasion they have fought valiantly in the field, and even led troops to victory.

THE RAJPUT REGIMENTS, WITH THEIR BATTLE HONOURS

2nd Queen Victoria's Own Rajput Light Infantry.

Badge.—The Royal and Imperial Cypher of Queen Victoria within the Garter.

Battle Honours.—"Delhi 1803," "Leswarree," "Deig," "Bhurtpore," "Khelat," "Afghanistan," "Maharajpore," "Punjab," "Chillianwallah," "Goojerat," "Central India," "Afghanistan 1879/80," "Burma 1885/87," "China 1900."

Uniform.—*Scarlet,* facings *blue.*

4th Prince Albert Victor's Rajputs.

Battle Honours.—"Leswarree," "Bhurtpore," "Kabul 1842," "Ferozeshah," "Sobraon," "Afghanistan 1879/80," "Burma 1885/87."

Uniform.—*Scarlet,* facings *black.*

7th Duke of Connaught's Own Rajputs.

Badge.—The Duke of Connaught's Crest and Cypher.

Battle Honours.—" Moodkee," " Ferozeshah," " Aliwal," " Sobraon," " China 1858/59," " Egypt 1882," " Tel-el-Kebir," " Pekin 1900."

Uniform.—*Scarlet*, facings *yellow*.

8th Rajputs.

Battle Honours. — " Sobraon," " Afghanistan 1879/80."

Uniform.—*Scarlet*, facings *yellow*.

13th Rajputs. (The Shekhawati Regiment.)

Battle Honours. — " Aliwal," " Afghanistan 1879/80," " Chitral."

Uniform.—*Scarlet*, facings *blue*.

16th Rajputs. (The Lucknow Regiment.)

Battle Honours.—" Lucknow " (with a Turreted Gateway), " Afghanistan 1879/80," " Burma 1885/87."

Uniform.—*Scarlet*, facings *white*.

THE MAHRATTAS

For geographical reasons connected with facility in recruiting, the Mahrattas are divided into two parts: the Konkani Mahrattas and the Dekhani Mahrattas. The whole race was originally confined to the country known as Maharashtra, but since their rapid acquirement of power in India they have spread beyond the limits of that country. They may now be found in the heart of the Central Provinces on the east, Central India on the north, and on the borders of Rajputana to the north and west.

Mahrattas are generally divided into three classes:—

1. Brahmans.
2. Chatris—*i.e.*, those who claim Rajput descent.
3. Sudras—those belonging to agricultural and trading classes.

The best of the soldiers are probably those recruited in the Dekhan, who are short, hardy and brave. Most of the Mahrattas in our ranks are recruited from the Konkan. They are taller and smarter than the Dekhanis, who, nevertheless, excel in endurance. The hillmen are nearly always more hardy than the inhabitants of the plain.

There is no history of the early Mahrattas, but as it is tolerably clear that the Mahratta language is Aryan, it follows that the race has at least Aryan blood, although ethnologists set it down clearly to be of Turanian or Dravidian origin.

It seems a curious thing that the Mahrattas were not brought up from the cradle of their race as fighting men, since they have proved in our first meetings with them such excellent foes. It is certain that if they are not born fighters, they have become good soldiers. Mr. Grant Duff in his "History of the Mahrattas" distinguishes them very clearly in a military sense from the Sikhs and the Gurkhas, while admitting that they make excellent soldiers. "The very fact of their having played so conspicuous and not always ignoble a part in the history of India," he says, "marks them out as a race with some qualities of the genuine soldier. The Duke of Wellington, who had such ample opportunities of forming a judgment in regard to them, rated them highly; and there can be no doubt that, with the discipline which the British officer enforces, and his personal example of courage, constancy, and devotion to duty, the Mahrattas can still be made into good soldiers, despite the enervating and softening influence which a long spell of peace appears to have on India."

Authoritative historians have said that the

courage of the Mahrattas of old was the courage of the freebooter; that they were at the best bold buccaneers, who were capable at times of courage because it paid them, but that the moment the prospect of gain was taken away, their courage oozed out. These writers maintain that the highest instincts of the soldier were never theirs. The reason of that was necessarily that the loyal and steadfast adhesion to a good cause, which has led the highest human types, in all ages, willingly to sacrifice their lives, never inspired them. Consequently, they were devoid of that spirit which takes death with proud indifference from motives of patriotism. One of these writers says: "The Mahrattas all through history have never sacrificed a whole skin unless there was something very tangible and substantial to be got thereby." Neither has Britain. We have never sacrificed, and never intend to sacrifice, our men for anything less than "something very tangible and substantial to be got thereby." The criticism on both sides then simply amounts to this: that courage is not a thing in itself, but a quality depending on motive, with knowledge; and the Mahratta, although he may have lacked both in the past, has certainly acquired them now.

Again, it has been contended that the Mahratta lacks the elegant proportions of the Jat Sikh, the robust, well-knit figure of the Gurkha, the lofty personal courage of the Pathan—in short, that he is cast in a mould that is anything but heroic. But, when we come to consider that there is in the Mahratta an essential sturdiness and tenacity, we find eventually, and apart from all superficially striking characteristics, the pabulum out of which the finest soldiery can be made.

In physique, the Mahratta is somewhat under the average height. His skin is dark, and his features irregular. But in those features one can discern a tremendous capacity for endurance. He may not be a cultured man—either falsely or truly—but, in the ranks, he possesses those natural adjuncts to steady, quiet strength, tractability, gentleness, patience, and a general willingness to fall in with the idea of someone who obviously knows more.

The Mahrattas in the 1st Bombay Infantry (Grenadiers), now the 101st Grenadiers, proved their grit at Maiwand. In a tough fight they held good till more than half their number were gone. Again, at Suakin, in 1885, the Mahrattas in the 28th Bombay Infantry (Pioneers), now the 128th Pioneers, proved, without a doubt, the nature of the qualities already mentioned, which will indubitably find further development in the present state of war.

Like the Rajputs, the Mahrattas are chiefly Hindus. They have strange objects of worship, such as trees and snakes. Their deities are principally incarnations of Shiva, the Destroyer, such as Etoba and Kandoba. Like all the Hindus, they still maintain a strong belief in Spirit, and, like all races who, in their early stages, have clung to that belief in darkness, they have developed a broader knowledge, which has always walked arm-in-arm with superstition towards enlightenment. Yet, especially in time of war, the Mahrattas throw aside all caste prejudices, even eat in common among themselves, and are not unwilling to accept a drink from Tommy Atkins himself.

A BRIEF HISTORY OF THE MAHRATTAS

Various theories have been advanced as to the origin of the Mahratta-speaking races of Western India. It is a generally accepted idea that, though the higher classes are to some extent of Aryan blood, the majority of the people are descended from aboriginal tribes who settled in the country long before the Aryans commenced their emigration from the Oxus.

The Mahratta country extends from Bombay in the north to Goa in the south, and from the Indian Ocean in the west to the Central Provinces and the Nizam's Dominions in the east. The tract is divided into two well-defined portions by the Ghats, a chain of hills running parallel with the coast. The strip of country near the sea, from the mouth of the Taptee to Goa, is generally known as the Konkan, and was formerly infested with pirates and brigands. The table-land of the Dekhan to the west of the Ghats has been inhabited for numberless generations by cultivators, shepherds, and herdsmen, and it was not until the Mahomedan persecutions had driven these peasants into rebellion that they developed any warlike instincts, and became aware of their own capacity for conquest.

Considering the power to which they at one time attained, it seems remarkable that no mention should have been made of the Mahrattas in history from the time of the Mahomedan conquests in the thirteenth century to the reign of Aurangzeb. It would appear, however, that during this period the country on each side of the Ghats was divided into numerous Hindu principalities, which paid tribute to the Mahomedan Kings of the Dekhan and Golkonda, but were never really subdued. A Mahratta family of the Bhondle tribe, which claimed to be of Rajput descent, had been for many generations in the service of the Sultans of Bijapur. At the beginning of the seventeenth century, a son of this family, named Sivaji, turned brigand, and supported by his peasant followers, who rapidly developed into soldiers, commenced a series of daring raids in the rich plain country to the east

WITH THE EXPEDITIONARY FORCE, 1914.

of the Ghats. In 1664 Sivaji changed the scene of his operations to the coast, and sacked the town of Surat, carrying off booty to the value of a million sterling. The British factory recently established there by the East India Company was successfully defended by the merchants, supported by sailors from their ships, but the exploit excited general alarm, for Surat was not only a great emporium for trade, but the port at which Mahomedan pilgrims embarked for Mecca, and landed on their return to India.

By this time the Moghuls were thoroughly alarmed. The levying of the "chanth," or fourth share of the revenue, by the Mahrattas was seriously affecting their finances, for Sivaji's raids extended to the south, and as far to the east as Bengal. Large Moghul armies took the field against his followers, but on the whole with very little success. The Mahrattas were loose hordes of lightly-clad horsemen, who lived on fruit and grain. They were the Cossacks of India, ever hovering round camps and armies to carry off treasure, though unable to face the heavy-armed Moghuls in the open field. The latter, however, were generally very wanting in activity. Mahrattas could easily escape from fortresses if driven out by starvation, and few Moghul commanders dared to follow them into the winding paths of the Ghats, whither they would retreat, lest the Moghuls, in their turn, should be cut off or starved into submission. Meanwhile, troops of Mahratta horsemen might be scouring the plains, harrying and plundering the peaceful villages, ready to gallop back at the first warning to their fastnesses in the hills and jungles.

Sivaji died in 1680, after a brilliant career of conquest. From then until 1707 the Mahrattas were weakened by quarrels among themselves, which caused the principal power in the state to be gradually transferred from the Bhonste descendants of Sivaji to a family of Brahmans, who were their hereditary Peishwas or Ministers.

Under these "Mayors of the Palace" the Mahratta power reached its zenith. Satara was their original capital, but there were powerful Mahratta governments established at Poona, Gwalior, Nagpur, Indore, and Baroda; and, towards the close of the eighteenth century, they started on a career of conquest which made them masters of India from Delhi to Cape Comorin—a career which was only checked by the rising power of the British.

"WILD MAHRATTA BATTLE"

At the time that the Mahratta Dominion was at its zenith in India, it came into clash with the ever-widening rule of the British. In 1803 the Mahratta Dominion extended from Hyderabad to Mysore as far as Delhi. In addition to this its dependencies and territorial possessions in India were far greater than those of the British.

The second Mahratta War was declared in August, 1803, and General Lake marched on Delhi. The British forces consisted of about 22,000 men in two equal divisions, one under Lake and the other under Wellesley, but the Mahrattas outnumbered this little force by seven to one.

The first event of the war was the attack on the fortress of Aligati by Lake. Here our men had a foretaste of the nature of "wild Mahratta battle" and of the terrible valour of the enemy. History records that the Mahrattas "fought like lions," and it was not until 2,000 of their number were slain that they finally surrendered. During the following week came the fall of Delhi, after a most determined conflict raged in sight of its minarets—a conflict in which the enemy lost 3,000 killed and wounded and 68 guns. A month later the famous stronghold of Agra was taken. This was an important victory, as in those days Agra was practically the key to Northern India.

In this campaign it was fully recognised that the Mahrattas were men of good fighting quality. At the battle of Leswarree, when Lake was outnumbered and forced to retire to wait for his infantry and guns to come up, the prowess of the

Mahrattas came as a surprise to him. When some reinforcements arrived he attacked again with still greater determination. On this occasion his horse was shot under him, and his son, dismounting to offer his own horse, was severely wounded. At the same moment, Lake, turning as his son fell, felt a shot pass between his arm and his chest, which, if he had not moved, would have found its way through his heart. But Lake was a man of cool judgment and imperturbable courage. Mounting his son's horse, he surveyed the field of battle and quickly made up his mind to decide matters by the bayonet. Our troops greeted the word of command with a hearty cheer, and immediately the 76th, admirably supported by the Native Infantry Corps, swept down upon the enemy in a furious charge. But Lake's generalship was matched by that of the Mahratta Chief, who instantly ordered his cavalry to charge. It was a tense moment, and it was rendered dramatic by the sudden appearance of the British Dragoons galloping to the relief. "Horse and foot," says a historian, "met in one great shock of battle; sabre rang out against bayonet and musket flashed against pistol and carbine. A short period of indescribable *mêlée* ensued, in which the fate of the day was decided."

The Mahrattas were defeated. They were a foe as worthy in those days of our steel as they are now, our comrades-in-arms, worthy of the Empire they defend.

Meanwhile Wellesley in the south was trying conclusions with Madhi Scindia and the Rajah of Madhpur. In conjunction with Col. Stevenson he had 7,000 men, who chased Scindia for three weeks, the wily chief having decided to fight on chosen ground. At length, on September 23rd, 1803, Wellesley, after a fatiguing march, reached the bank of the Kaitna River. He was waiting for Col. Stevenson, with whom he had prearranged a plan, but when he discovered that the enemy was in camp on the other side of the river, he concluded that his chance of bringing Scindia to action was "now or never." Accordingly he resolved not to wait for Stevenson, but to attack at once. This was a daring decision, for Scindia's forces numbered 17,000 foot, of whom 10,500 were highly disciplined infantry ; and his artillery, consisting of the regular equipment supplemented by 115 guns, was far stronger than that of the British. In addition to this his Mahratta Horse numbered about 30,000. The little British army that was getting ready to defeat this gigantic force numbered 4,520 men, of whom 1,170 (74th and 78th Regiments) were British Infantry, 2,000 Native Infantry, 1,200 Cavalry, and 150 Artillery. The Mahrattas saw this piece of audacity and stood awhile in amazement, but, wise in their generation, they forbore to call the force opposing them "contemptible." When the rest of the world came to have something to say about it, Wellesley simply remarked: "But had I not attacked them I must have been surrounded by their superior cavalry, my troops had starved and I had nothing left but to hang myself to my tent-pole." But it may be justly contended that it was not wholly a case of Hobson's choice, for Wellesley, like Nelson, knew when to be rash and how to be rash, and it might have been said of him, in the words of the French Admiral about Nelson, that his genius lay in the fact that he could rightly estimate every weakness of his enemy.

The battle which followed was of a terrible and terrific nature, but it ended eventually in a glorious victory for the British. From first to last, Wellesley, having conspired with the luck of war, left no single point to the luck of chance.

From an elevated plain he could see the whole Mahratta force encamped on the north side of the Kaitna, where the banks of that river were very steep. Their right, consisting of cavalry, extended to Bokerdon; their left, consisting of infantry, with ninety pieces of artillery, lay near the village of Assaye, which has given its name to the memorable battle.

Wellesley resolved to attack the infantry on its left and rear, and for that purpose he moved his little army to a ford beyond the enemy's left, leaving the Mysore and other irregular cavalry to watch the Mahratta cavalry, and crossing the river only with his regular horse and infantry. He passed the ford, ascended the steep bank, and formed his men in three lines—two of infantry, and the third of horse. This was effected under a brisk cannonade from the enemy's artillery. Scindia, or the European officer who directed his movements, promptly made a corresponding change in his line, giving a new front to his infantry, which was now made to rest its right on the river and its left upon the village of Assaye and the Juah stream, which flowed in a parallel direction with the Kaitna. Scindia's numerous and well-served cannon did terrible execution among Wellesley's advancing lines, killing men and bullocks, and drowning the weak sound of his scanty artillery. At one moment such a gap was made by cannon-ball in the English right that some of the Mahratta cavalry attempted to charge through it; but the British cavalry in the third line came up and drove the Mahrattas back with great slaughter. Finding his artillery of little or no use (the guns could not be brought up for lack of bullocks), Wellesley gave orders to leave it in the rear, and bade the infantry charge with the bayonet.

His steady, resolute advance in the teeth of their guns had already awed the Mahrattas, who would not stand to meet the collision of the

English steel: their infantry gave way, and abandoned the guns. One body of them formed again, and presented a bold front; but Lieutenant-Colonel Maxwell charged them with the British cavalry, broke and dispersed them, and was killed in the moment of victory. Wellesley's Sepoys having proceeded too far in pursuit, many of Scindia's artillerymen, who had thrown themselves down among the carriages of their guns as though they were dead, got to their feet again, and turned their pieces against the rear of the advancing Sepoys; and at the same time the Mahratta cavalry, which had been hovering round throughout the battle, were still near. But Maxwell's charge soon silenced the desultory artillery fire, and Scindia's disciplined infantry went off and left ninety pieces of cannon, nearly all brass and of the proper calibres, in the hands of the victors. Wellesley led the 78th British infantry in person against the village of Assaye, which was not cleared without a desperate combat.

Assaye cost Wellesley twenty-two officers and 386 men killed, and fifty-seven officers and 1,526 wounded. Excluding the regular cavalry which had remained on the other side of the river and had not been engaged, the total number of killed and wounded amounted to nearly one-third of his force. The general himself had two horses killed under him, one shot and the other piked; every one of his staff officers had one or two horses killed, and his orderly's head was swept off by a cannon-ball as he rode close by his side. The enemy, who had fled towards the Adjuntee Ghat, through which they had poured into the Dekhan, left 1,200 dead, and a great number badly wounded on the field of battle.

THE MAHRATTA COMPANY REGIMENTS, WITH THEIR BATTLE HONOURS

Although there are no Class Regiments composed wholly of Mahrattas, they form in Company Regiments the bulk of the following bodies of Infantry:—

103rd Mahratta Light Infantry.

Raised 1768.

4 companies Dekhani Mahrattas, 2 companies Konkani Mahrattas, 2 companies Dekhani Mussalmans.

Battle Honours.—"Mysore," "Seedaseer," "Seringapatam," "Beni Boo Alli," "Punjab," "Mooltan," "Goojerat," "Abyssinia."

Uniform.—*Scarlet,* facings *black.*

105th Mahratta Light Infantry.

Raised 1788.

4 companies Dekhani Mahrattas, two companies Konkani Mahrattas, 2 companies Dekhani Mussalmans.

Battle Honours.—"Mysore," "Seedaseer," "Seringapatam," "Beni Boo Alli," "Kahun," "China 1860/62," "Afghanistan 1879/80," "Burma 1885/87."

Uniform.—*Scarlet*, facings *black*.

110th Mahratta Light Infantry.

Raised 1797.

4 companies Dekhani Mahrattas, 2 companies Konkani Mahrattas, 2 companies Dekhani Mussalmans.

Battle Honours.—"Central India," "Abyssinia," "Afghanistan 1879/80."

Uniform.—*Scarlet*, facings *black*.

114th Mahratta Light Infantry.

4 companies Konkani Mahrattas, 2 companies Dekhani Mahrattas, 2 companies Dekhani Mussalmans.

Uniform.—*Scarlet*, facings *yellow*.

116th Mahratta Light Infantry.

Raised 1800.

4 companies Konkani Mahrattas, 2 companies Dekhani Mahrattas, 2 companies Dekhani Mussalmans.

Battle Honours.—"Afghanistan 1879/80," "British East Africa 1901."

Uniform.—*Scarlet,* facings *yellow.*

117th Mahratta Light Infantry.

4 companies Konkani Mahrattas, 2 companies Dekhani Mahrattas, 2 companies Dekhani Mussalmans.

Uniform.—*Scarlet,* facings *yellow.*

There are companies of the Mahrattas also in the

107th Pioneers.
108th Infantry.
109th Infantry.
121st Pioneers.
128th Pioneers.

THE GURKHAS

THE Gurkha is more closely a brother-in-arms to Tommy Atkins than is any other native soldier. These brave little men swell with pride—and their chest expansion is enormous—when they are referred to as the "Highlanders of India." Their eyes twinkle and their white teeth gleam in a smile of joy at this well-deserved honour bestowed upon them for many a valiant fight. To stand by the side of their big brothers of the Black Watch, the Seaforth, the Gordon, the Cameron, and the Argyll and Sutherland Highlanders in glory and renown is their Nirvana of bliss; and now, in the greatest conflict of Europe, to fight, and if need be to die, in the same line with them for the great King-Emperor (the Padisha), in the defence of the world against tyranny and wrong, is absolutely the crowning moment in the history of this valiant little man of Nepal. As the Gurkha marches to-day to the tune of The Marseillaise, played on a weird collection of instruments approaching as nearly as possible to the bagpipes, his cheerful spirit is glad beyond words to be in line with the heroes who claim his special admiration, and his one thought is " Shall we fight side by side with the Gordons, as we did at Dargai, or with the Argyll and Sutherland Highlanders, or with the Seaforths ? "

But behind his cheerful countenance and jaunty way of carrying himself lies a bulldog courage which, in turn, commands the admiration of his big brothers-in-arms—the British Highlanders. Those gleaming teeth are exposed in no kind of smile when he grips the deadly *kukri* in a hand-to-hand encounter, and there is no twinkle in the fierce black eyes as he sets his face to the foe, with the cool determination " never to go back," which is a tradition of his race.

On this point, Lt.-Col. Newnham-Davis, writing in " Town Topics," declares that " The Gurkha is the most thorough little man I have ever met in campaigning ; he will never go back. He tackles any job that is given him like a bulldog, and he is never beaten. In manœuvres, as in action, one thing a Gurkha regiment will not do is to go back.

" I have seen the Chief Umpire and all his satellites vainly trying to explain to the native officers of a Gurkha company on manœuvres that they were surrounded and outnumbered and out of action, and that they must therefore retire from the mimic fight. The Gurkhas grinned and stopped where they were, and it was only by sounding the 'cease fire' and telling the little men to get back and cook their dinners that the Chief Umpire moved them off the ground."

"In the spring," says the Colonel, writing on the Gurkha War, "the little Gurkhas—jovial little fellows, broad-chested and big-limbed, short in stature, with their Tartar eyes, noses like pugdogs, and great good-natured gashes for mouths—flock down to enlist in our regiments. Brave as lions, vain as peacocks, faithful as dogs, with few prejudices in peace and none in war, the Gurkhas are the special friends and companions of our men.

"The stately Sikh throws away his food if a white man's shadow falls upon it, and between the Mahomedan and the Christian is always the bar of religion, but on a campaign the Gurkha eats his food with as few formalities as Tommy Atkins drinks his wine, and is good company at the camp-fire."

The Gurkha has a merry wit and an equally happy conceit, as the following incident will show. After the assault on Bhurtpore, where the Gurkhas raced with the grenadiers of the 59th for the bridge, the British soldiers praised them for their bravery. They returned the compliment by the following characteristic remark: "The English are as brave as lions; they are splendid Sepoys, and *very nearly* equal to us."

It may be seen from the above incident that the vanity of these little men is colossal. Indeed, it is only exceeded by their loyalty and gallantry, which can never be questioned, since Lord Roberts, the hero of Kabul, has accorded them the highest and warmest praise.

When Col. Younghusband, travelling in the Pamirs with an expedition of Gurkhas, met the great Russian explorer Gromschefski, a native officer of the Gurkhas asked leave to speak to Younghusband. "Tell him," he said, pointing to the big Russian, "that though *we* are small men, all the rest of our regiment are taller than he is."

The only ritual the Gurkha observes is that he washes his hands and face and takes off his head-dress before cooking his meals. Any meat that chances to come the Gurkhas' way they call *shika* (game). It is permitted by their religion to eat anything they have killed when hunting, but in their native land they prefer a kind of food made from rice. In the British service they take kindly but temperately to anything that the canteen supplies.

The Gurkhas were originally protectors of the cows, and this in India is a more or less Divine right. The Hindu regards the cow in the light of his mother, and frequently the beef-eating habit of the Sahib is pathetically reproached by the native in these terms: "What! would you eat your mother?" It may be permissible to stretch the derivation of their name in the present day and apply it to the fact that Britain is now their mother, and that they flocked westward to assist her in her great effort to uphold and ensure the integrity of the world.

The Gurkhas, or Gurkhalis, claim descent from the Ranas of Udaipur in Rajputana. Long ago, when they were driven out of their own country by the Mahomedan invasion, they sought refuge in the mountainous tracts about Kumaon. From this point they gradually began to invade the country to the eastward, as far as the city of Gurkha, Noakote, and ultimately the valley of Nepal, and even Sikkim. It was only when they attempted to force their way southwards that they were met and repulsed by the British. The Treaty of Segauli, which put an end to the Gurkha War of 1814, set a definite limit to their territorial expansion.

In general character the Gurkha is bold and self-reliant. On his gentler side, while extremely independent and self-centred, he is frank, faithful, and capable of fine, heroic loyalty. All his ideas of war and sport are modelled on European ideas. Though resembling in many ways the little Jap, he is built on far sturdier lines. As a humorist once remarked of his race: "They are 5 feet high in some places, and 5 feet round in others." Their movements in attack resemble lightning rapidity as nearly as anything human can. Essentially a phlegmatic race, they are supposed to lack sentiment and emotion, but education and touch with Western civilisation have proved to a great extent that these qualities were potential. In many ways they have been brought out as true sentiment and emotion of the steadier and more genuine kind. This fact, with their natural gaiety of disposition and their good-humoured carelessness of good or evil hap, is no doubt the reason that they make such fine soldiers. There is no grumbling on the part of the Gurkhas.

The Gurkha in battle is terrible, and almost weird in his methods. His ways are the ways of no other living soldier. And this brings us to a consideration of that remarkable weapon, the *kukri*. It is a heavy, curved knife, as sharp as a razor, and its drawing cut, inflicted with much skill and little force on anything in motion, has terrible effects. For instance, the intrepid Gurkha will wait for the tiger of the jungle to spring, and then, at the right moment, will step aside, leaving his deadly knife to follow the movement of his arm across the tiger's throat.

This wonderful knife, which the Gurkha loves as the British gunner loves his gun, has a small hilt, such as is common to all Indian swords. The blade is about nine inches long, and has a point as sharp as a needle. Both the hilt and the blade are curved, so that the weapon does equally well for the drawing cut or the thrust. Owing to the extreme thickness of the broad blade the weapon is remarkably heavy—a property devised obviously for the purpose of gaining the full force of inertia when the *kukri* is wielded by the dexterous hand and wrist of the Gurkha. One authority on this weapon says that the weight of the razor-edged blade would drive it half through a man's arm if it were only allowed to fall from a little height. One can imagine, then, the terrible effect if used for the drawing cut of the broad-sword. In the Gurkha's experienced hand its sharp edge carves through both bone and sinew, proving it to be a weapon as formidable as can be conceived. The method of this little warrior with the *kukri*, then, may be described as an inhibition of force and an exhibition of skill, for by means of it he will quickly cut to pieces any man of gigantic strength and build who does not understand his mode of attack.

Many years ago, during the conquests on which we founded our Eastern Empire, our men frequently came into clash with the Gurkhas. In those days they were, as enemies, as formidable as they are to-day invaluable as brothers-in-arms. Here is a description of one battle incident in which we suffered severely at their hands :

" Brave as lions, active as monkeys, fierce as tigers, the wiry little men came leaping over the ground to the attack, moving so quickly and keeping so far apart from each other that rifle fire was of little use against them. When they came near our soldiers they suddenly crouched and dived under the bayonets, striking upwards at our men with their *kukris* and ripping them open with a single blow, then darting off as rapidly as they came." Until our men learnt this mode of attack they were greatly discomfited by their little opponents, who got under their weapons, cutting or slashing with knives as sharp as razors, and often escaping unhurt from the midst of the bayonets.

In all the history of invasion and conquests, of floating dynasties and mushroom empires in the East, the most sanguinary chapters deal with the British subjugation of the Gurkhas.

At a time when the Gurkhas were only some twelve thousand strong their reputation as fighters stood high. Many a time and oft had they raided neighbouring territory, carried off cattle, and even extorted tribute, so that at length the British authorities realised that there was only one course to take, and the message was sent to the bold Gurkha Chief: " Keep within your own territory or beware of the consequences." But this ultimatum was treated with scorn by the Gurkhas. Their haughty spirit could not brook such a demand. Hot blood seethed in their veins, and hot words were spoken at their council meetings. Their natural warlike spirit rose to the occasion and they declared war.

That war of 1813-14, and that conquest of a truly warlike race, form a record of one of the most heroic achievements of the British Army.

Nepal, the home of the Gurkhas, is situated on the slopes of the Himalayas. Its natural barricade on the north is a mighty line of peaks soaring against the sides of heaven up to the roof of the world, covered with everlasting snow. In front and to the south dense forests protect it from the approach of an invading host. Terrible were the difficulties and hardships of our men in these forests. Despair almost drove them back, while the prospect of utter failure seemed to stare them in the face. But, as if in a forlorn hope, our men went on, toiling and moiling towards the borders of Nepal; and, with the tenacity that saves every hopeless situation, gained at length the walls of Kalanga.

The fort held out for a long time, but fell at length, though not until the heroic garrison of six hundred had been reduced to seventy. It was here that brave General Gillespie fell as he was cheering his men forward to a fruitless attack. At the outset he had reckoned upon an easy conquest, but owing to the staunch resistance of the Gurkhas, reinforced by their natural advantages, he found the greatest difficulty.

There are many incidents recorded of the Gurkhas in this war, but perhaps the following is characteristic. When a party of our troops were searching for the enemy's outposts, they happened to fall in with a band of Gurkhas. The fierce little men raised a yell and produced their deadly *kukris* ; then, after a brief consultation, their leader strode forward into the open and challenged the English officer in command to a settlement by single combat. His challenge was no sooner offered than it was accepted, and Captain Showers advanced to meet him. A short, sharp fight then took place on the plain separating the two opposing forces; steel met steel, and, after a quick passage, the Gurkha's blood ran crimson in the snow. He had met one who knew his methods.

This war dragged slowly and wearily to a close. Finally there came a time when the Gurkhas were compelled to sue for peace. By the treaty drawn up at the conclusion of hostilities large tracts of territory were ceded to the British ; but, as this treaty had to be sent to the Governor-General for approval and signature, there was a delay, and during that delay the bold spirit of the Gurkhas rose against this admission of defeat, and when the treaty was returned they flatly refused to sign it. At this hostilities were resumed, and the British again proceeded to attack.

This time they had a larger share of the luck of war. By the guidance of a party of smugglers they were enabled to penetrate right into the Gurkha stronghold unobserved. Their path lay through deep ravines, darkly enclosed by rugged precipices and shrouded in the gloom of dense overhanging trees. Threading their way through these eerie approaches, they at length came up behind the Gurkhas, who were patiently waiting and watching the regular avenues of approach. Being suddenly attacked in the rear, the Gurkhas were demoralised, and, though they fought bravely, were defeated. This action proved decisive. Again they were conquered, and, from that time, they have nobly admitted the superiority of their conquerors. A few years later their indomitable spirit was linked with that of the British, and they were fighting side by side with the white man in Asia.

The Gurkhas of to-day adhere to the Hindu religion. In their appearance there is a strong trace of Mongolian blood, as shown by their almond-shaped eyes, high cheek bones, and firm but mobile lips.

In early times Nepal consisted of a great number of petty states constantly at war with each other. Thus it happened that, by conquest and re-conquest, and intermixture of tribes, the term "Gurkha" became geographical rather than ethnic; that is to say, the name does not, strictly speaking, apply to any special tribe or race, but to the inhabitants of the locality known as Gurkhá.

The principality of Gurkhá owes its existence and name to a yogi called Guraknath. He lived in a cave in a hill in Central Nepal. To this holy man came many devotees daily, and, in the neighbourhood of his cave, there soon sprang up a village which in time spread its boundaries until it assumed importance as the City of Gurkhá, so named after the yogi. In further course of time it became the capital of the district, to which, and to its inhabitants, it gave its name.

It is interesting to note that this yogi Guraknath is still held in great veneration by all Gurkhas, and to-day their battle-cry may be heard in Europe—" Guru Guraknath Kijai " (" Victory to Guraknath ! ").

The Gurkhas are conquerors of no mean order. Their principal conquests took place in the middle of the eighteenth century. In the year 1599 Drabiya Sah elected himself Gurkha Rajah, and, about 140 years later, the eighth in descent from him—one Narbupal Sah—invaded the Nepal valley. The invasion was unsuccessful and he was driven back, but the spirit of invasion was not defeated. He was succeeded in 1742 by his son, Prithwi Narayan Sah, a lad twelve years old. This boy grew up into a sensible, brave man of great ambitions, and in time became a very capable general and diplomat. It was to his genius as a ruler and a general that the Gurkhas owed their ultimate conquest of the region of Nepal. His first invasion failed, though he and his warriors fought with splendid courage. Later, having subjugated several of the neighbouring states, he strengthened his army from these sources, and undertook a second invasion in 1765. Again he was utterly defeated: but he was a man of heroic courage, and, in his third invasion in 1768, in the course of which he was defeated as often as he was successful, he finally seized Khatmandu—by superior "strategy" as it was known in those days—and dictated terms of peace in the heart of the valley of Nepal.

Prithwi, the conqueror, then removed his capital to Khatmandu, which has ever since remained the capital of the Gurkha kingdom. He died in 1775, after a great and terribly eventful reign of thirty-three years.

Pratap Simha Sah, who succeeded his father Prithwi, attempted the conquest of Sikkim, but failed utterly. In Sikkim the Maharajah obtained the victory over him in so many battles that the Gurkha king was forced to sign away some of his eastern territory; but the Gurkhas returned again and again to the attack, until, in 1776, they utterly defeated the Sikkim Maharajah at the battle of Chinepore, and more than regained their lost possessions.

In 1776 the wars of conquest still continued. Another great man arose, Ran Bahadur Sah, uncle to Pratap Simha Sah's infant son, who was on the throne. Bahadur Sah was a man of ability, and, as Regent, decided to subjugate the Chaobisi principalities. He conspired with the Rajah of Palpa, one of the Chaobisi states, agreeing to a division of the spoil in return for his assistance. The Gurkha-Palpa alliance was then formed, and nearly all the Chaobisi states were subjugated, the Gurkhas keeping the lion's share. Meanwhile the Gurkha armies in the east, under General Saroop Simha, were victorious, and the whole of the Rai and Limbu districts of eastern Nepal were conquered. For some time after that they continued the extension of their rule in Sikkim and parts of Tibet. This latter invasion brought upon the Gurkhas a strong Chinese army, which utterly routed them in the year 1792. In consequence of this the Regent was executed by order of the infant king, who himself, on account of his later atrocities, was forced to abdicate in 1800. After some years of exile in India he returned as a firebrand to Gurkha, and died unhonoured and unmourned in 1807.

It was during the second and third Afghan wars that the Gurkhas and the Highlanders fought together in an admirable combination. A brief description of these two wars, containing some graphic incidents of battle, and showing the part the Gurkhas and the Highlanders played together, will be found in the following chapter.

SOME BATTLES IN WHICH THE GURKHAS HAVE FOUGHT

It is interesting to trace to-day the heroic exploits of the Gurkhas through campaigns in which they have fought side by side with the Highlanders of our own country. Space admits of only a brief account, but it will serve to show exactly how and why the Arms of Lord Roberts come to bear, as supporters, a Highlander and a Gurkha.

The second Afghan war (1878-80) was brought about by the discovery of Russian intrigues with Shere Ali. Although the Amir had been advised by Lord Lytton that he was sending Sir Neville Bowles Chamberlain on a mission to Kabul, he made no satisfactory reply either in assent or dissent; but when Sir Neville reached Ali Musjid, a fortress on the Afghan frontier, his embassy was confronted by an armed force, and, not possessing sufficient troops to attack, he was compelled to turn back. Smarting under this affront—for it had been clearly laid down that his mission was not of a hostile nature—he returned to Peshawur, from which point an ultimatum was despatched to Shere Ali. This led to the formal proclamation of war on November 21st, 1878. Ali Musjid was the scene of the first battle, in which, under Sir Samuel Browne, the 6th Native Infantry, the 45th Sikhs, and 27th Punjab Infantry were engaged.

Prior to this battle the Kurram Column, or Field Force, had been formed, under General Roberts. The native troops included in this force were as follow :—

1ST INFANTRY BRIGADE—29th Bengal Native Infantry, 5th Punjab Infantry, and the Bhopal contingent.

2ND INFANTRY BRIGADE—21st Native Infantry, 2nd Punjab Infantry, and 5th Gurkhas, under Major Fitzhugh.

This famous Kurram Column immediately took the field, and their first engagement of importance was at Peiwar Kotal. To the 29th Bengal Native Infantry and 5th Gurkhas, under Col. Gordon, No. 1 Mountain Battery, a wing of the 72nd (Duke of Albany's Own) Highlanders, the 2nd Punjab Infantry and 23rd Pioneers, under Brigadier Thelwall, was assigned the task of turning the enemy's position, while a feint was to be made upon their front. The turning force set out during the night of December 1st. A writer who describes that campaign says : " The bright camp-fires shed their wavering light on the white tents, when, without sound of drum or bugle, the troops fell silently into their ranks, the companies were told off, and the battalions formed. . . . Nor had they long to wait before their challenge was responded to by two shots, showing that the position had been reached. And ere long the troops found themselves confronted by an abattis formed by felled trees which, laid over each other to the height of 8 feet, completely blocked the way."

On this barricade, the Gurkhas, led by Major Fitzhugh and Captain Cook, made a fierce rush. A stern conflict ensued—a hand-to-hand fight with bayonet, *kukri*, and clubbed musket; and the Gurkhas drove the enemy back to a second barrier nearly 100 yards to their rear. Here they made another stand, but the ferocity of the lithe and wiry Gurkhas, and the stern valour of the Highlanders—their right wing falling upon the enemy's flank—combined to drive the Afghans from this second stockade with considerable loss.

Here it was that the Gurkhas and the Highlanders rushed on together side by side in a memorable charge, none of them knowing the strength and number either of the enemy or his further stockades. In the uncertain light of early dawn they drove the enemy up the hillside like chaff before the wind. For a time the Afghans fled in disorder, then suddenly they rallied and prepared for a wild charge downhill. Major Galbraith of the 85th Foot was the first to see their intention, and he immediately directed the fire of his men to demoralise and check this movement. While he was doing this an Afghan crept up behind some bushes, and, levelling his rifle at him, took careful aim. Suddenly the Major observed him, and, with the rapidity of lightning, raised his revolver and pulled the trigger. The weapon missed fire, but his prompt action had disturbed the Afghan's aim, and in another moment Captain Cook of the Gurkhas had closed with the native and flung him heavily. There was a quick fight between them, during which Major Galbraith, more fortunate this time with his revolver, sent a bullet through the Afghan's heart. For his brave act in saving the Major's life Captain Cook gained his V.C. But the nation was compelled to mourn this hero very soon, for it was in the following campaign at Sherpur, while leading the Gurkhas, that he was mortally wounded.

By the dawn of day the Gurkhas and the Highlanders, with the assistance of the 29th Punjabis, had taken some important positions, and by the time the sun rose the enemy was defeated.

This victorious campaign was carried on through the craggy ravines of Sappri as far as

Siafooden, where the Afghans made a stand and gave battle a second time; but here again the Gurkhas and the Highlanders were the principal factors in their defeat. The subsequent brilliant rush on Shaturgardan Pass was also made glorious by these Highlanders of Britain and Asia. The campaign ended on May 26th, 1880.

Again, in the third Afghan war, the Gurkhas, in common with different regiments of High landers and some native regiments, won great distinction.

Sir Louis Cavagnari, who had concluded peace after the first campaign, undertook a personal mission to Kabul. This time the mission was well received—at least at first—but there soon came a time when the Afghans, taking advantage of the necessary inferiority in the numbers of our peaceful mission, insulted it, at first vaguely, then openly, apparently with the idea of goading the Governor to a quarrel. Insult on insult gave fuel to the fire thus aroused, and at last, when the insults became unbearable, the Governor and his staff protested so vigorously that the Afghans seized their opportunity and massacred them. Immediately following on this came the declaration of war by Shere Ali. After the preliminary battles at Charasiah and Asmai the British force advanced to Kabul. There was very severe fighting around the capital, and another sharp engagement at Asmai, after which our troops found themselves entrapped in Sherpur. Here the Gurkhas won a lasting glory for themselves by the recapture of some of our guns which had been taken by the enemy.

During this campaign the Gurkhas took part in the battle of Sijazabad. Here the enemy took up a strong position on the side of a steep hill, which they had further strengthened by barricades of earth and stone. From one to another of these they were driven point by point by the determined assault of the 4th Gurkhas, 14th Punjabis, and the 9th Foot. This was a battle in which all our outnumbered forces, especially the Gurkhas, showed remarkable *élan*. For many hours the Gurkhas stormed one barricade after another, always driving the Afghans up the hill with bullet, bayonet, and *kukri*, until at last the enemy's final defence was taken. It was in this battle that an incident occurred which shows, not only the Gurkha's quality, but his primitive methods of revenge—which methods, needless to say, are now somewhat modified. Towards the close of the uphill battle, when the enemy was in full retreat, a single Gurkha, in advance of his fellows, had just shot one of the Afghans, when two of them suddenly sprang up from behind a rock near by. They were Afghan hillmen—fanatics pledged in the name of Allah to the last drop of blood for Islam. They shared the belief, common among Orientals, that death under this pledge was the entrance to Paradise, where the houris are born of pure musk. With a spring one of them fiercely plunged his dagger into the unfortunate Gurkha, while the other with a sweep of his tulwar clove the head of the dying man. Swift as was this passage of arms, still swifter came the retribution. Lieut. Gordon of the 92nd Foot despatched one of the hillmen, and the other immediately fell, riddled by Gurkha bullets. With a ferocious cry the Gurkhas swept down upon the two stricken hillmen, and with their terrible *kukris* hewed them in pieces. But as the time of Samuel and Agag has departed, so has this primitive lust of revenge been gradually modified in the Gurkha by his association with the humanity of the West.

The Gurkhas were in the famous march of General Roberts on Kandahar, which immediately followed the battle of Sijazabad. It was towards the end of this march that the Gurkhas and the 92nd Gordon Highlanders made an attack on the little village of Gundi-Moolah-Sahibdad. In this memorable assault the Gurkhas and the Gordons almost strove with one another for the *kudos* of the victory. But the *kudos* may easily be said to belong to them jointly. And in recognition of this the Gordon loves to talk about his little comrade-in-arms, while the Gurkha worships the Gordon to such a degree that he would lay down his life for him.

The Afghan strife closed—let us hope for ever—with the battle of Kandahar. This conclusive fight stands in history as a signal tribute to the tenacity of the British soldier in general, and to the generalship, since tried and proved and never found wanting, of Lord Roberts. Says a historian, "It was remarkable for the generalship and cool judgment Roberts had shown, and also for the courage displayed by his troops. . . . On every occasion we were far outnumbered by the enemy, who were equal to our men in physical strength, and armed with nearly the same weapons; but Roberts trusted to the courage of his slender army and to its perfect discipline, which were conspicuous alike in the savage defiles of the Kurram Valley, on the rocky heights of the Peiwar Kotal and the Spingawi Pass, in the lines of Sherpur, and on the splintered bluffs of Asmai."

The Kandahar Field Force was disbanded in September, 1880, and Roberts' last act before returning to India was to distribute distinguished-service medals to the 72nd and 92nd Highlanders and the 5th Gurkhas. These are his words on that occasion, and no doubt every Gurkha at the front to-day has them, or their translation, in his memory, for they have, more than anything else, confirmed and ratified a brotherhood-in-arms between the Gurkhas and the Highlanders :—" Soldiers of the Kandahar Field Force, I am glad to have this opportunity of giving medals for distinguished conduct to the men of the 72nd and 92nd Highlanders and the 5th Gurkhas. They have deservedly won them. I say from my experience as a soldier that no men with whom I have served can have better deserved these rewards ; and it is an additional pleasure to me to have seen the other day of what material my Highlanders and Gurkhas are made. I can but hope it may be my good fortune to have such good soldiers at my side when next I go into action. . . . You may be assured that the very last troops the Afghans ever wish to meet in the field are the Scottish Highlanders and the Gurkhas."

After this, from one who is now a veteran of England, who can doubt that, as the Gurkhas marched towards the front, their hearts went before them to their big brothers of former frays, with the hope that they would be in close touch in the battle line ?

THE GURKHA REGIMENTS, WITH THEIR BATTLE HONOURS

The following is a complete list of the ten Gurkha Regiments (each composed of two battalions), with their Battle Honours, etc. :—

1st King George's Own Gurkha Rifles

(The Malaun Regiment).

Raised at Subathu in 1815, chiefly from Gurkha soldiers of Amar Singh, by Lieut. R. Ross.

Badges.—The Plume of the Prince of Wales and the Royal and Imperial Cypher.

Battle Honours.—"Bhurtpore," "Aliwal," "Sobraon," "Afghanistan '78/80," "Punjab Frontier," "Tirah."

Uniform.—*Dark green*, facings *scarlet*.

2nd King Edward's Own Gurkha Rifles (The Sirmoor Rifles).

Raised at Nahau (Sirmoor) in 1815, by Lieut. F. Young, from Gurkha soldiers, who took service with the British on the termination of the first phase of the Nepal war. Granted a truncheon for distinguished service at Delhi, 1857.

Badges.—The Plume of the Prince of Wales and the Royal and Imperial Cypher of Edward VII.

Battle Honours.—"Bhurtpore," "Aliwal," "Sobraon," "Delhi," "Kabul '79," "Kandahar '80," "Afghanistan '78/80," "Punjab Frontier," "Tirah."

Uniform.—*Dark green*, facings *scarlet*.

3rd Queen Alexandra's Own Gurkha Rifles.

Raised at Almora in 1815, by Lieut. Sir R. Colquhoun, Bart., from Gurkha soldiers, who took service with the British after the fall of Malaun and the conquest of Kamaon; supplemented by transfers from the Gorakhpur Hill Regiment, and originally designated the Kamaon Battalion.

Badge.—The Cypher of Queen Alexandra.

Battle Honours.—"Delhi," "Ahmad Khel," "Afghanistan '78/80," "Burma '85/87," "Chitral," "Punjab Frontier," "Tirah."

Uniform.—*Dark green*, facings *black*.

4th Gurkha Rifles.

Raised in 1857, by Lieut. D. Macintyre, as an extra Gurkha regiment.

Battle Honours.—"Ali Masjid," "Kabul '79," "Kandahar '80," "Afghanistan '78/80," "Chitral," "Punjab Frontier," "Tirah," "China 1900."

Uniform.—*Dark green*, facings *black*.

5th Gurkha Rifles (Frontier Force).

Raised at Abbotabad in 1858, by Capt. H. M. F. Boisragon, as the 25th Punjab Infantry, or Hazara Gurkha Battalion.

Battle Honours.—"Peiwar Kotal," "Charasiah," "Kabul '79," "Kandahar '80," "Afghanistan '78/80," "Punjab Frontier."

Uniform.—*Dark green*, facings *black*.

6th Gurkha Rifles.

Raised at Chanbiaganj (Cuttack) in 1817, by Capt. S. Fraser, as the Cuttack Legion. Subsequently the 42nd Gurkha Rifles. Present designation, 1903.

Battle Honour.—"Burma '85/87."

Uniform.—*Dark green*, facings *black*.

7th Gurkha Rifles.

Raised at Thayetmyo in 1902, by Major E. Vansittart, as the 8th Gurkha Rifles; became 2nd Battalion of the 10th Gurkha Rifles in 1903. Present designation, 1907.

Col.—Field-Marshal H. H. Viscount Kitchener of Khartoum.

Uniform.—*Dark green*, facings *black*.

8th Gurkha Rifles.

Raised at Sylhet in 1824, by Capt. P. Dudgeon, as the 16th or Sylhet Local Battalion; 1st

Battalion was subsequently known as the 44th, 2nd Battalion as the 43rd. Present designation, 1903.

Battle Honour.—" Burma '85/87."

Uniform.—*Dark green,* facings *black.*

9th Gurkha Rifles.

Raised at Fategarh in 1817, by Major C. F. Fagan.

Battle Honours. — " Bhurtpore," " Sobraon," " Afghanistan '79/80," " Punjab Frontier."

Uniform.—*Dark green,* facings *black.*

10th Gurkha Rifles.

Raised in 1890, by Lt.-Col. C. R. Macgregor, from the Kubo Valley Police Battalion, and originally known as the 10th Regiment of Burma Infantry.* Present designation, 1903.

Uniform.—*Dark green,* facings *black.*

* It is a singular fact that the old 10th Madras Infantry (1st Burma-Gurkha Rifles), raised in 1766, bore the honours " Carnatic," " Mysore," " Amboor," " Assaye," " Ava," " Burma '85/87," and in 1900 Capt. J. Henegan was a wing commander. He is now, at the time of writing, Lieut.-Col. commanding the 1st Battalion of the present 10th Gurkha Rifles.

Another peculiar point will recommend itself to military students. In " Whitaker's Naval and Military Directory" of 1899 and 1900 the 17th and 19th regiments of Madras Infantry are given, but the 18th regiment is omitted. This, however, is not the only instance of the kind. As in the case of our 5th (Royal Irish) Lancers there have been certain regiments that have disappeared for a time from the Army List, the numbers of the others remaining unaltered.

THE DOGRAS

THERE is some little doubt about the derivation of the word "Dogra." Some say it is derived from the Indian word "dogur" or "dugur," meaning "hill" or "mountain," and that the Dogra country is so called because the whole of it is more or less mountainous. Others maintain that the origin of the name is found in two Sanscrit words, "do," meaning "two," and "girath," meaning "lake," there being two small lakes of great beauty known as Man Sur and Sardin Sur. The first derivation is most probably the correct one, for it is a matter of history that the pioneer Rajputs, who left the plains to make their home in the hills to found the Dogra principalities, styled themselves Dogras, or Hillmen, as distinguished from men of the plains.

The district of Dogra lies between the rivers Chenab and Sutlej, including all the hills and valleys on the slopes of the Western Himalayas.

The Dogra is a shy, reserved man, with considerable strength of character. He may not be so brilliant as the Pathan, nor so tenacious and subtle as the Gurkha, but he has a high idea of honour, is very self-respecting, and makes a capital soldier. Since he is always ready to cast aside his social prejudices he affords recruiting officers little trouble. The virtues of this solid, quiet, resolute, reliable man are seen in moments of peril, when, without any boasting or striking of attitudes, he will face certain death with a calm determination to do before he dies.

From the above description it will be gathered that the Dogra is simple-minded and generous, capable of the highest loyalty, and a complete stranger to anything like treachery or cruel barbarity. It is through the combination of all these qualities that the Dogras as a race have justly earned, and faithfully maintained, the reputation of being among the best fighting material to be found in India.

The Dogra's physique is not so fine as that of the Pathan or Sikh. He is a man of average height, somewhat sparely built, with fine, sensitive features. His complexion is fair, though not as fair as that of the Todas.

The Dogras are very particular in all matters relating to food and drink. They are keen sportsmen, and in rifle-shooting they maintain a fair standard of excellence. Hawking and snaring birds are favourite pastimes among them, and even such games as tip-cat, leap-frog, and hop-scotch are not unknown to them.

This brave and loyal race were faithful to us during the Mutiny, and their services at the siege of Delhi were invaluable; but as early as 1849 their soldierly qualities had been recognised, for it was at that time that the Government enlisted great numbers of them in the Punjab Frontier Force. The reason of this lay chiefly in their military value, although it was at the same time evident that they would be useful to balance the influence of the Sikhs, who were still imbued with Khalsa traditions.

The 2nd Sikh Infantry, raised at Kangra in 1846, consisted entirely of Dogras. This was the regiment that ratified its loyalty by assisting to quell a rebellion of its own countrymen. Later, in the second Afghan war, this same regiment, the majority still being Dogras, fought gallantly at the battle of Ahmad Khel. Indeed, there was a moment in this battle when victory or defeat depended entirely on this regiment. At this critical juncture it behaved splendidly, and disaster was averted.

THE DOGRA REGIMENTS, WITH THEIR BATTLE HONOURS

Company Regiments—Cavalry

It must be borne in mind that Company Regiments are those which contain squadrons or companies of different native classes. The following regiments of Indian Cavalry contain Dogras in the proportions given:

7th Hariana Lancers, one squadron.
9th Hodson's Horse, half a squadron.

10*th Duke of Cambridge's Own Lancers* (Hodson's Horse), one squadron.

11*th King Edward's Own Lancers* (Probyn's Horse), one squadron.

12*th Cavalry*, one squadron.

13*th Duke of Connaught's Lancers* (Watson's Horse), one squadron.

16*th Cavalry*, one squadron.

19*th Lancers* (Fane's Horse), half a squadron.

21*st Prince Albert Victor's Own Cavalry* (Frontier Force) (Daly's Horse), half a squadron.

23*rd Cavalry* (Frontier Force), half a squadron.

25*th Cavalry* (Frontier Force), one squadron.

Class Regiments—Infantry

37th Dogras. Raised 1858, disbanded 1882, re-formed 1887.

Comprises 8 companies of Dogras.

Battle Honours.—"Chitral," "Punjab Frontier."

Uniform.—*Scarlet*, facings *yellow*.

38th Dogras. Raised 1858.

Comprises 8 companies of Dogras.

Battle Honours.—"Punjab Frontier," "Malakand."

Uniform.—*Scarlet*, facings *yellow*.

41st Dogras. Raised 1900.

Comprises 8 companies of Dogras.

Uniform.—*Scarlet*, facings *yellow*.

THE BALUCHIS

THE Baluchis are said to come of Arab stock. Their legends and traditions attribute their origin to Hamzah, an Arab of the Koreish tribe, which claimed the honour of including the prophet Mahomet as one of its number. Mahomet is said to have been Hamzah's nephew. Notwithstanding the fact that some Mahomedan peoples are in the habit of employing elaborate fiction in their claims to close connection with their prophet, it still remains that there is much evidence in favour of the general tradition existing among the Baluchis as to their Arab origin.

The traditional Hamzah, progenitor of the Baluchi race, is regarded as one of the most important of the early Mahomedan chiefs. He is pictured as a mighty warrior, a man of Herculean strength and high courage; hence his romantic and classical sobriquet, "Lion of God." The tradition runs that Hamzah was killed at the battle of Ohod in 625 A.D. His descendants and adherents settled about Aleppo, whence they were driven by Yezid, son and successor of Muavia, and first Omeyeid Kalif. It seems that the reason for this expulsion was that Hamzah and his tribe had given assistance to Hössein, grandson of the prophet, in his attempt to oust Yezid from the position which he had occupied.

Being driven forth into the desert, the tribe migrated eastward as far as Persia, where, as pastoral nomads, they wandered and lived and multiplied to such an extent as to cause considerable alarm to the Persian monarch. It is to this sojourn that the Baluchis attribute their obvious admixture of Persian blood and characteristics. As their rapid increase in numbers promised trouble to the Persian kingdom, steps were taken to expel them, and they ultimately descended into an uninhabited tract south-east of Mekran—a country to which no one laid any definite claim. From this point they gradually spread over the whole of the country now known as Baluchistan, driving before them all the peoples who had so far emigrated to that region. It will be seen from this that the probabilities are decidedly in favour of the Arab origin of the Baluchis. Yet it has been contended by some that they are a race of Turkish stock, since certain of their rites and customs seem to be drawn from that source; nevertheless it is more probable, from all the available facts, that the Turcoman and Persian characteristics and survivals are merely the result of a temporary admixture.

The Baluchis

Very little is known of the early history of the warlike Baluchis beyond what can be drawn from tradition, unsupported by any written historical records. One of their chief traditions is that Jalal Khan, who led them out of Persia, had four sons, named Rind, Hot, Lashari, and Korai; and a daughter named Jato. At the present day there are five distinct tribes which still bear the names of these five children of Jalal Khan; but of these tribes the Rind and Lashari soon acquired, by reason of their superior force of character, a predominant influence, so that, as the people multiplied and split up into an ever-increasing number of tribes, all these fell under the domination of the Rind or the Lashari. Gradually in this way all the Baluchi race came to be divided under two great heads, the Rind and the Lashari—a division which has been determined, not by descent, but by political sympathy.

The Rind division possess a great traditional hero, Mir Chakar, who is supposed to have lived in the sixteenth century, and to have been a powerful dependent of the Moghul Emperor Humayun, giving him great assistance in his re-conquest of the Delhi throne. In return for this Humayun bestowed upon Mir Chakar a large tract of land on the frontier, and it is more than probable that the Baluchis' settlements on the southern frontier were founded in this way.

The Lashari faction also had their traditional hero, Mir Gwahram Khan, of whom many stories of heroism are recorded. His name has still a sound of glory for the Lasharis.

The Baluchis follow the Mahomedan religion, but, like the Gurkhas, they are not religious by nature, preferring practical pursuits and tangible material ideals, chief among which is war. It is not that they are less bigoted than many of the other races, but rather that they are more practical. Their language is a rude and far-off dialect of the early Persians, and they have no form of written literature.

Although the Baluchi differs greatly from the Pathan in the matter of religion, there are many points in common in regard to social character. The Baluchi has the manly, frank, brave, strong nature of the Pathan, with a fund of patience rendering him capable of enduring endless hardship, and a fine dignified carriage and physique combined with a spirit of quick daring and sudden ferocity; to these qualities he adds the virtues of truth, fidelity, and simple generosity. His condemnation of servility, insolence, deceit, and treachery in many tribes is indicative of his character. His wild, free, open-air life, combined with the artificial restraints of civilisation, has given him a bold and resolute air of vigour and self-reliance. It redounds to his fundamental integrity to find still existing in

Baluchistan a kind of altar or sacred stone—"a stone or cairn of cursing—erected as a perpetual memorial to the treachery of one who betrayed his fellow." His chivalry is superior to that of some more cultured races, for, wild as he is, he will not harm the women and children even of his bitterest foe. Yet his moral code allows him to plunder and to loot on a wholesale scale. But set against this is his strong adherence to discipline, a quality which has developed more and more during his closer touch with the British.

If a Baluchi were allowed his own choice of weapons in any fight whatever, his immediate selection would be a long knife, a sword, and a shield. He has never found any material use for the matchlock, which has always been so dear to the heart of the Pathan. He is a born knifer, and loves to kill at close quarters—a fact based upon the primitive blood-thirstiness of his nature, "blood for blood" being his motto. The tales of the Baluchi's prodigal hospitality to a stranger within his gates, and then way-laying and murdering him on his departure, must be discredited in these days, when these fierce instincts have been turned into worthier channels. Nor should any credence be accorded to such stories of degradation as picture him the habitué of the opium, hemp, and gambling dens; for, though he may have been prone to wild excesses, recent years have seen nobler ambitions placed before him, and certainly those Baluchis now showing their loyalty and love for Britain and the right on the battlefields of Europe are not of the class of whom these stories have been told. A word of praise must be given to the Baluchi's horse, which he rides as if it were a part of him. Baluchistan produces some of the finest horses in the world.

THE BALUCHI REGIMENTS, WITH THEIR BATTLE HONOURS

Cavalry

37th Lancers. (Baluch Horse.) Raised 1885.

Class Squadron Regiment. 2 squadrons Derajat Mussalmans (including Baluchis), 1 squadron Pathans, 1 squadron Sikhs.

Uniform.—*Khaki serge*, facings *ouff.*
(No service.)

Infantry

126th Baluchistan Infantry. Raised 1825.

Class Company Regiment. 2 companies Hazaras, 1 company Khattacks, 1 company Waziris, 2 companies Baluchis and Brahmans, 2 companies Sikhs and other Jat Sikhs.

WITH THE EXPEDITIONARY FORCE, 1914.

Battle Honours.—" Persia," " Khooshab," " China 1900."

Uniform.—*Drab* (*red serge trousers*), facings *scarlet*.

127th Queen Mary's Own Baluch Light Infantry. Raised 1844.

Class Company Regiment. 4 companies Pathans, 2 companies Hill Baluchis, 2 companies Punjabi Mussalmans.

Badge.—In each of the four corners the Cypher of Queen Mary.

Battle Honours.—" Delhi," " Abyssinia," " Afghanistan 1878/80," " Burma 1885," " British East Africa 1897/99."

Uniform.—*Green* (*red serge trousers*), facings *scarlet*.

129th Duke of Connaught's Own Baluchis. Raised 1846.

Class Company Regiment. 4 companies North-west Frontier Pathans, 2 companies Hill Baluchis, 2 companies Punjabi Mussalmans.

Battle Honours.—" Persia," " Reshire," " Bushire," " Khooshab," " Kandahar 1880," " Afghanistan 1878/80," " Egypt 1882," " Tel-el-Kebir."

Uniform.—*Green* (*red serge trousers*), facings *scarlet*.

130th King George's Own Baluchis.

(Jacob's Rifles.) Raised 1858.

Class Company Regiment. 3 companies Pathans, 2 companies Mahsuds, 3 companies Punjabi Mussalmans.

Badges.—The Plume of the Prince of Wales and the Royal and Imperial Cypher.

Battle Honours. — "Afghanistan 1878/80," "China 1900."

Uniform.—*Green* (*red serge trousers*), facings *scarlet.*

THE BATTLES OF THE GOLDEN DAGON PAGODA

(Burmese War, 1824)

DIMINISHED by sickness and death, brought on by hard service during an inclement season, by defective provisions, and by the ordinary casualties of war, Sir Archibald Campbell's forces at Rangoon were greatly weakened. But the opportune arrival of the 89th British Regiment from Madras, and of parts of two detachments which had subdued the islands of Cheduba and Negrais, raised the effective strength just at the critical moment. By the end of June, 1824, the Burmese in this quarter appeared to have somewhat recovered from their defeats at our hands. Chiefs of the highest fame, who, until they came in contact with our troops, had always been victorious, were sent down the Irawaddi from Ava and from Prome, with orders to slay or torture and mutilate every Burmese soldier that did not fight to the utmost; and one of the brightest of golden umbrellas, Sykya Wongee, minister of state, was appointed commander-in-chief, with positive commands from the Golden Foot to attack and drive the British at once into the sea. Following this, on the first day of July, all the woods in Sir Archibald's front exhibited bustle and commotion; 8,000 men had crossed to the Rangoon side of the river; the jungles around all seemed animated; clouds of rising smoke marked the encampments of the different corps of the Burmese army in the forest; and their noisy preparations for attack formed a striking contrast to the still and quiet of our readiness.

Golden Dagon Pagoda was the key of the British position. This splendid edifice, in itself a fortress, is a little over two miles from the town of Rangoon. In shape it resembles an inverted speaking-trumpet; it is 338 feet high, and is surmounted by a cap made of brass, 45 feet high; the whole is richly gilded. The base of this pagoda is a conical hill, flat at the top, and rising about 75 feet above the road.

In the neighbourhood of this gorgeous building Sir Archibald Campbell placed a whole battalion of British troops. The two roads running from the pagoda to the town were occupied by our forces, native and European. The minor pagodas, bronze houses, and pilgrims' houses along these two roads afforded good shelter to the troops against the stormy weather, and some further shelter from the attack of an enemy whose artillery was somewhat light. Two detached posts completed our position—one at the village of Puzendown, about a mile below the town, where the Pegu and Rangoon rivers meet; the other at Kemmendine, about three miles above the town; this second post being chiefly intended to protect our shipping against the descent of the enemy's fire-rafts.

On the morning of July 1st the enemy issued in dense masses from the jungle to the right and front of the Golden Dagon Pagoda. Detaching to their left a column, which succeeded in setting fire to part of the village of Puzendown, their main body came boldly up to within half a mile of Rangoon, and commenced a spirited attack upon part of our line. But two field-pieces, served with grape and shrapnel, presently checked their advance, and then a brilliant charge by the 43rd Madras Native Infantry put them all to flight. In a very few minutes not a man could be seen of the Burmese host, except the killed and wounded; nor could anything be heard of them except a wild screaming of baffled fury coming from the depths of the forest.

Their defeated commander was brought to book by the Golden Foot, and degraded. Then a still higher minister of state, named Soomba Wongee, who had arrived with reinforcements, took the command, and commenced stockading his army in the most difficult and intricate part of the forest, at Kummeroot, about five miles from the Great Pagoda, intending, chiefly under cover of night, to carry on such a system of desultory warfare as would harass, and ultimately destroy, our sickly, worn-out soldiers. He also fortified a commanding point on the river about Kemmendine, in communication with his stockaded camp, hoping by this means not only to obstruct the navigation of the river, but also to construct and employ numerous fire-rafts. But this new commander-in-chief had scarcely finished his works when he was driven from them with a terrible slaughter.

It was on July 8th that Sir Archibald Campbell embarked with one column for the attack of the position upon the river, and Brigadier-General MacBean, with a land column, marched upon the forest stockades at Kummeroot. The works on the river were found to be so formidable that it was judged necessary to employ breaching vessels; accordingly a brig and three Company's cruisers, manned by seamen of his Majesty's and the Company's navy, under the superintendence of Captain Marryat, soon opened a heavy cannonade and silenced the enemy's guns. Our troops then pushed across the river in boats, entered the practicable breach which the firing of our seamen had made, and carried all those works with comparatively trifling loss. The Burmese suffered severely in killed, and many of them were drowned in trying to escape across the river.

The operations of the land column, under MacBean, were equally successful. It was unprovided with artillery; but the storming parties, who escaladed stockade after stockade, consisted entirely of British troops. Here, again, the slaughter was dreadful. Soomba Wongee, and several chiefs of high rank, with 800 men, were killed within the stockades; and the neighbouring jungles were filled with the unhappy creatures who were wounded, and left to die from want of food and care. Some of these poor Burmese were found by the English soldiers, and brought into our hospitals; but, unfortunately, none of them recovered. The monsoon rains were now at their height. The adjacent country was almost wholly under water. Nothing was to be obtained from it. Again, disease spread so rapidly among our troops that the outlook was desperate.

Meanwhile an Expeditionary Force, consisting of his Majesty's 89th Regiment and the 7th Madras Native Infantry, under the command of Colonel Miles, was detached from Rangoon, with a considerable naval force, to subdue the maritime possessions of his Burmese Majesty to the eastward, in the hope that their loss might induce him to sue for peace. The success of the expedition was complete: Tavoy surrendered. Mergui was taken by storm, and British protection was welcomed by the inhabitants of the entire coast of Tenasserim.

Some few weeks later Sir Archibald Campbell attempted to release such of the inhabitants of Rangoon as were desirous of returning to their houses; and, by means of the sudden, unexpected, and, to the natives, inexplicable movement of our steamboats, a few families who had been driven to the villages at the heads of the numerous creeks which branch off from the Rangoon river were released from their guard, and joyfully took the opportunity of returning to their city. It was to the report of these people of the kind treatment they met with that our army was afterwards indebted for the return of the great body of the men whose services and exertions contributed to the final success of the war.

Having, so far, failed in all his undertakings, the Lord of the White Elephant now sent his two brothers, the Prince of Tonghoo and the Prince of Sarrawaddy, with a whole host of astrologers and a corps of "Invulnerables," to join the army and to direct the future operations of the war. The astrologers were to fix the lucky moment for attacking; the "Invulnerables" had some points of resemblance to the Turkish Delhis; they were the desperadoes, or madmen, of the army, and their madness was kept up by enormous doses of opium. The corps consisted of several thousand men, divided into classes; the most select band of all being called the "King's Own Invulnerables."

Battles of Golden Dagon Pagoda

The Prince of Tonghoo established his head-quarters at Pegu, and the Prince of Sarrawaddy took post at Donoopew, upon the great river, about sixty miles from Rangoon. In the beginning of August the Prince of Sarrawaddy sent down a force to occupy a strong post at the mouth of the Pegu River, a few miles below Rangoon, giving his people strict orders to block up the channel of the river in our rear, so that not one of the " wild foreigners " or " captive strangers " might escape the punishment that was about to fall upon them. Brigadier Smelt was at once sent, with a small corps, to dislodge Sarrawaddy's force. Our land troops were brought to a stand-still, when within musket-shot of the place, by a deep and impassable creek ; but a party of sailors from his Majesty's ship *Larne,* under Captain Marryat, threw a bridge over the creek ; and, as soon as the column of attack pushed forward, the enemy began to fly, leaving eight guns and a quantity of ammunition in their stockade. A strong pagoda, with a numerous garrison, and with cannons pointing down every approach, was next carried with equal facility. Other posts on the rivers and creeks were then attacked and taken. Such of the enemy as had had any experience of our way of fighting seldom stopped to fight in their stockades ; but a new set of people from the interior made a good stand in a succession of stockades on one of the rivers, and cost us the loss of a good many brave men.

All this time the astrologers were busy casting the lucky moment. Finally they told the Prince of Sarrawaddy that the moment had come for a decisive action; and, on the night of August 30th, a body of the "King's Own Invulnerables" promised to attack and carry the Golden Dagon Pagoda, in order that the princes and the sages and pious men in their train might celebrate the usual annual festival in that sacred place—which was now crowded with English grenadiers. And, true so far to their promise, the "Invulnerables," at the hour of midnight, rushed in a compact body from the jungle under the pagoda armed with swords and muskets. A small picquet, thrown out in our front, retired in slow and steady order, skirmishing with the "Invulnerables" until they reached the flight of steps leading from the road up to the pagoda. The moon had gone down, and the night was so dark that the enemy could be distinguished only by a few glimmering lanterns in their front; but their noise and clamour and the volume of their threats and imprecations launched upon the impious strangers if they did not immediately evacuate the sacred temple proved their number to be very great.

"In a dense column," says the historian, "they rolled along the narrow pathway leading to the northern gate of the pagoda, wherein all seemed as silent as the grave. But hark! the muskets crash, the cannons roar along the ramparts of the British post, drowning the tumult of the advancing column; and see!—see by the flash of our guns, the column reels back, the 'Invulnerables' fall, mortally wounded, and the rest turn their backs on the holy place, and run with frantic speed for the covering of the jungle."

Our grape-shot and our musketry broke the spell—those "Invulnerables" ventured no more near any of our posts. But a far more terrible enemy came within the lines; the dysentery broke out among our troops, killing many of them, and reducing more to a most emaciated and feeble state. Scarcely three thousand duty soldiers were left to guard the lines. Floating hospitals were established at the mouth of the river; and bread was now furnished in sufficient quantities, but nothing except change of season or of climate could restore the sufferers to health. Mergui and Tavoy, portions of our conquest on the sea-coast, were represented by the medical officers who visited them as admirable convalescent stations; and thither a number of our soldiers were sent, and with the most beneficial result. Men who had for months continued in a most debilitated state at Rangoon, rapidly recovered on arriving at Mergui, and were soon restored to their duty in full health.

The Lord of the White Elephant now determined to call down from the mountains of Arracan his prime favourite, and to carry off the Governor-General in golden chains. Bandula obeyed the call, and led his reinforced army from the mountains of Arracan to the Irawaddi river. He had begun his march about the end of August, at a season of the year when none but Burmese could have kept the field for a week, much less have attempted to pass the unhealthy jungles and the pestilential marshes of the country. The distance, by the shortest route, was more than 200 miles ; but Bandula, gathering fresh forces in the latter part of his long march, reached Donoopew before Sir Archibald Campbell knew that he had left Arracan. Happily, our troops, though woefully reduced in numbers, were now fast recovering their health and strength ; and two fresh British regiments, some battalions of native infantry, a regiment of cavalry, and a troop of horse artillery arrived from Calcutta and Madras, together with some admirable trotting cattle of the true Mysore breed. Five hundred native boatmen came round from Chittagong, and were busily employed in preparing boats for river service.

The rains had now ceased at Rangoon ; and Sir Archibald Campbell, strongly reinforced, was completing his preparations for the ascent of the Irawaddi, and for an attack upon Prome, when he learned that Bandula had reached Donoopew with 60,000 fighting men, a considerable train of artillery, and a body of Cassay horse, the best cavalry in this part of Asia. Bandula's musketeers were estimated at 35,000 men. Other numerous bodies were armed with gingals, which carried an iron ball of from six to twelve ounces, and were mounted on a light carriage easily dragged about by two men; and great numbers were attached to the guns which were transported on the backs of elephants. The rest of the host were armed with swords and spears, and scattered through the army were more of the "Invulnerables" who had not yet tasted the sour grape of English guns, and who were amply provided with charms, spells, opium, bhang, and betel-nuts. As Bandula proclaimed on all sides his intention of riding at the head of his invincible army, with horses and elephants and all manner of warlike stores, to capture and destroy the British at Rangoon, it was deemed proper to wait for him there with a view to a decisive battle.

The enemy came down to the neighbourhood of Rangoon in boats. Our posts, consisting of redoubts and fortified pagodas, were speedily constructed, connecting the great Golden Dagon Pagoda by two distinct lines with Rangoon and the river, and leaving a disposable force for moving to the support of any point that might require such support. The post at Kemmendine was also strongly occupied, and was supported on the river by his Majesty's sloop *Sophie*, Captain Ryves, a Company's cruiser, and a strong division of gunboats.

On November 30th Bandula's great army assembled in and behind the dense forest; and his line, extending from the river above Kemmendine in a semicircular direction towards Puzendown, might be distinguished by a curved line of smoke rising above the trees. During the ensuing night the low, continuous murmur and hum of voices proceeding from the enemy's encampment suddenly ceased, and were speedily succeeded by the distant but gradually approaching sounds of a multitude in slow and stealthy movement through the woods. Our troops soon became aware that the enemy's masses had approached to the very edge of the jungle, within musket-shot of the pagoda, apparently in readiness to rush from their cover to the assault at the break of day.

The day had scarcely dawned on December 1st when hostilities commenced with a heavy fire of musketry and cannon at Kemmendine, the reduction of that place being a preliminary to any general attack upon our line. The firing continued long and brisk, and from their commanding situation at the Great Pagoda, though nearly two miles distant from the scene of action, our men could distinctly hear the yells and shouts of the infuriated assailants, occasionally returned by the hearty cheer of the British seamen as they poured in their heavy broadsides upon the resolute and persevering masses. The thick forest which separated us from the river shut out all sight of what was going forward; and, when the firing ceased, we remained. There was a short period of anxiety, though little doubt as to the result of the long and spirited assault. At length, however, the thick canopy of smoke which lowered over the fierce and sanguinary conflict gradually dissolved, and there could be seen the masts of the vessels lying at their old station off the fort—a convincing proof that all had ended well on that side.

Meanwhile the enemy had been seen on the west side of the river, marching across the plains of Dalla towards Rangoon. They were formed in five or six different divisions, and moved with great regularity, led by numerous chiefs on horseback—their gilt umbrellas glittering in the rays of the sun—with a sufficiently formidable and imposing effect. Opposite Rangoon the leading column of five or six Burmese divisions began entrenching and throwing up batteries, while their main body was stockading in the jungle. In the course of the day several heavy columns issued from the forest, and successively took up their ground along a woody ridge, gently sloping towards Rangoon. Here they commenced operations with their entrenching tools, and with such activity and good will that in the course of a couple of hours their whole line was covered; their flags and banners, which had been flying in profusion, all disappeared, and nothing was seen but a parapet of fresh-turned earth, gradually increasing in height. The moving masses, which had so very lately attracted anxious attention, had sunk into the ground; and, by anyone who had not witnessed the whole scene, the existence of these subterranean legions would not have been credited. The occasional movement of a chief with his gilt umbrella from place to place, superintending the progress of their labour, was the only thing that now attracted notice. By a distant observer the hills, covered with mounds of earth, would have been taken for anything rather than the approaches of an attacking army. Even to those who had watched the whole strange proceeding, it seemed the work of magic or enchantment. But, thus working like moles in the earth, the Burmese could no more see than they could be seen; and, in the afternoon, Major Sale, with his Majesty's 13th Regiment and a regiment of Madras Native Infantry, moving rapidly forward upon the busily employed and too confident enemy, fell upon them before they were well aware of the visit, and drove the whole line from their earthworks with considerable loss.

These Burmese trenches were found to be a succession of holes, capable of containing two men each, and excavated so as to afford shelter both from the weather and the fire of any enemy ; even a shell lighting in the trench could at most kill but two men. As it was not the Burmese system to relieve their troops in making these approaches, each hole contained a sufficient supply of rice, water, and even fuel for its inmates ; and under the excavated bank a bed of straw or brushwood was prepared, in which one man could sleep while his comrade watched. When one line of trench was completed, its occupiers, taking advantage of the night, would push forward to where the second line was to be opened, their places being immediately taken up by fresh troops from the rear, and so on, progressively. The Burmese understood this art of warfare, but our men—especially our Native Infantry—also understood that art, and the enemy's weaknesses as well.

Attacks were made on Kemmendine that day and were all repulsed by our troops or by the seamen of our little flotilla. But it was not until night that the Burmese made their last desperate effort to open their way down the river, and so get possession of the port of Rangoon. The soldiers had lain down to rest, when suddenly the heavens and the whole surrounding country became brilliantly illuminated. The enemy had launched their fire-rafts into the stream with the first of the ebb-tide, and had now applied the match to those huge masses of combustible materials, in the hope of driving the *Sophie* and our other vessels from their stations off Kemmendine ; and as these fire-rafts came down, it was seen by the light of their flames that they were followed by a vast fleet of war-boats, whose crew were ready to take advantage of the confusion which might ensue if any of our vessels should be set on fire. As the rafts floated rapidly down to Kemmendine with the ebbing tide, columns of attack moved once more by land against that well-defended post, with artillery, gingals, and musketry.

But the skill and intrepidity of British seamen proved more than a match for the numbers and devices of the Burmese ; after gazing for a while at the red, blue, yellow and green flames of the mighty fireworks, our sailors leapt into their boats, pushed off to meet the flaming rafts, secured them with their grappling irons, and conducted them safely past our shipping or ran them ashore to finish their short but vivid life of fire and flame upon the river bank without injury to anyone. If these fire-rafts could have reached the harbour of Rangoon, which was now crowded with transports and vessels of all kinds, the effect might have been very tragic ; but the British tars said that none should pass Kemmendine Point, and none did pass. Kemmendine, where the river makes a sudden turn, was the only point from which the rafts could have been launched with effect. Fully aware of this, Bandula ordered attack upon attack to be made, and for seven days no rest by night or by day was allowed to our troops or to our seamen there. But every effort of the enemy failed—even their land attack on Kemmendine.

On December 5th, when the stores of the Burmese left wing were brought forward from the jungle to their foremost entrenchment in front of Rangoon, and were fairly within our reach, Sir Archibald Campbell ordered a decisive attack to be made upon their army. Major Sale, with one column 800 strong, and a troop of British dragoons, who had only been landed the preceding day, was directed to fall upon their centre ; and Major Walker, with 500 men, was sent to make a vigorous attack on their left wing. The operations of these two columns of troops were greatly facilitated by Captain Chads of the navy, who proceeded up the Creek to a point within gunshot of the rear of the enemy's line, with the man-of-war boats and a part of the flotilla, and began a heavy cannonade which distracted the attention of the Burmese and prevented their strengthening their front. Our two columns broke through the entrenchments, and completely routed both the centre and the left with vigorous bayonet charges ;

but Major Walker and a good many of his gallant comrades fell. The loss of the Burmese was appalling; they were driven from every part of their works into the jungle, leaving the ground behind them covered with dead and wounded, with all their guns, entrenching tools, gilt umbrellas, and a great number of small arms. On December 6th, Bandula tried to rally his defeated troops, and with some success. On the 7th the Burmese made their last and grand attack on the Great Pagoda, but they were beaten, driven back to their entrenchments by the British bayonet, and finally into the depths of the jungle.

Our troops at that post, worn out by seven days and nights of incessant fighting and watching, could not pursue the flying enemy, who left in the trenches a great number of dead—nearly all stout, tall, athletic fellows, who might almost have measured with English grenadiers, and who had evidently belonged to the flower of Bandula's army. During these seven busy and fiery days the Burmese, in addition to a prodigious loss of life, had lost every gun and their entire stores. The survivors fled towards Donoopew, but they were stopped in their flight by some great and terrible chiefs, who had been sent down with numerous reinforcements, and they rallied at Kokeen, about four miles beyond the Great Pagoda.

It is said that when Bandula counted his

forces he found them reduced from more than 60,000 fighting men to less than 25,000. Nevertheless, this favourite of the Lord of the White Elephant was allowed to retain the chief command. His first move was to entrench and stockade himself at Kokeen, after which he employed incendiaries to burn the invaders out of Rangoon, and destroy all their stores and powder magazines. On the night of December 12th the cry of fire resounded through the town of Rangoon, and nearly the whole of that flimsy, bamboo-built place seemed to be immediately in a blaze. The incendiaries had placed their matches in various parts of the town, and had set fire to them all the same moment. One half of the town was burned; but the flames were prevented from reaching our depot of stores and ammunition. This attempt, which was very nearly successful, brought down a rapid attack upon Bandula's new position, and defeat and ruin upon himself. On December 15th—three days after the midnight fire at Rangoon—1,500 British troops and sepoys, unaided by artillery, under the command of Brigadier-General Willoughby Cotton, drove Bandula and his mighty host from all their entrenchments and stockades at Kokeen, and strewed the position with his dead in thousands.

BHURTPORE

(1826)

If any fortress in India could have been with good reason called impregnable, that fortress was Bhurtpore. In the early years of the nineteenth century the chiefs and rajahs of Hindustan were wont to say, "Yes, you may bully us, but go and take Bhurtpore!" Their belief in its impregnability was well founded, for in 1805 Lord Lake had attacked it vigorously, but had failed to reduce its well-fortified works manned by staunch and numerous defenders. After suffering terrible losses he was compelled to withdraw, leaving this Jat fortress with a still stronger claim to impregnability than it had ever possessed before.

When it was once decided by the British Government that Bhurtpore must fall, the question immediately arose, where was the man to take it? The East India Company Directors interviewed the Duke of Wellington, asking him to find a man capable of taking this fortress. The Duke gave them an answer. He said, "You can't do better than have Lord Combermere. He's the man to take Bhurtpore." "But," replied the directors with great surprise; "we thought that your Grace had not a very high opinion of Lord Combermere, and did not consider him a man of genius." "I don't care a tuppenny damn" (that was the Iron Duke's favourite par of exchange in hot words) "about his genius. *I tell you he is the man to take Bhurtpore!*" And the Duke was right.

There were 25,000 men in the Bhurtpore garrison, and they represented the most warlike races of India. When Lord Combermere set out with Bhurtpore as his objective, his army consisted of 30,000 men of very mixed quality. On reaching the fortress he began with heavy bombardment. Then for a week he carried forward his siege works, covered by Gurkha sharpshooters, whose eyes were so keen and whose aim so sure that no man of the enemy could show his head above the ramparts with impunity.

Point after point was won until, at last, a small breach was made by the artillery; and into this breach Lord Combermere flung a force in which were included 600 dismounted men from the various cavalry regiments—eighty from the 11th Light Dragoons, eighty from the 16th Lancers, 200 from Skinner's Horse, and forty from each regiment of native cavalry.

Skinner's Horse is one of the earliest formed of the many distinguished Native Irregular

Cavalry Corps which have fought for Britain. They had been under Colonel Skinner for many years, and had served him in many wars; thus they had come to respect and love him as tribesmen do their chief. There is a touching story of their valour and faithfulness during the storming of Bhurtpore. A party was told off according to rota duty, for the whole regiment had volunteered for the dangerous service. Skinner placed at their head Shadull Khan, one of his oldest, most faithful, and trustworthy native officers. Then he spoke to them as follows: "This is the first time you are going into danger when I cannot accompany you; but such is my affection for you all that I cannot allow you to part from me without carrying with you something dear to me." Then, taking his son by the hand—the lad had only lately entered the corps—he continued: "See, here is my son. Take him and gain for him such honour as you have won for his father."

This shows clearly what Colonel Skinner thought of Skinner's Horse, and also what he knew they thought of him. Old Shadull Khan stepped forward, and, taking young Skinner by the arm, cried out, "Farewell, our commander! Trust in God, who never deserts those faithful servants who do their duty and who, please God, will now do their utmost to maintain the honour of the corps."

Although the assault on the breach had been planned, it was postponed for that day, as on further consideration Lord Combermere deemed it was not practicable. It took place later, after a great explosion of mines which the engineers had placed beneath the ramparts. On entering the widened breach our troops encountered fierce opposition. There was a hand-to-hand fight of the most desperate description, and it was not until after some hours of fierce fighting that the enemy surrendered.

The Iron Duke's words were justified; Lord Combermere had taken Bhurtpore, and that successful assault on a fortress long regarded as impregnable was one which yields in brilliancy and courage to few in the British annals of war. Its beneficial effect on British rule and influence in India was as striking as its place among battles is dramatic.

THE WAR IN SCINDE

(Meeanee, 1843)

"LET there be sixty or a hundred thousand," said Sir Charles Napier, "I will fight."

This was when he moved away from the banks of the Indus and found that an overwhelming force of the enemy was massing in his rear, while another large force held Meeanee in his front. In the spirit of his words he pushed forward with 2,600 of all arms, including officers fit for duty in the field, and the result was the important battle of Meeanee.

The positions of the Baluchis were formidable. In the first place they had a natural ravine in their front. Again, they had 5,000 cavalry and more than 30,000 infantry, with fifteen guns. Their wings rested on dense woods which extended on each side of the plain in front for a considerable distance, so as to flank the British lines on both sides when it should advance. But, in no mood to be intimidated by these natural advantages of the enemy, Sir Charles Napier and his little force fell impetuously on him by the front. The fighting which ensued was terrific. Our men gradually forced their way across the level plain, swept as it was by the Baluchi cannon and matchlocks, and finally crossed the ravine and began the ascent of the high, sloping bank beyond.

With matchlocks laid ready in rest along the summit, the Baluchis waited until the assailants were within twenty yards before they discharged a volley. But the active British offered an uncertain mark, and this, combined with the steepness of the declivity, accounted for the inconsiderable result of their fire.

Now the 22nd (the Cheshire Regiment) were on the top of the bank, thinking to bear down all before them, but "they staggered back in amazement at the forest of swords waving in their front. Thick as standing corn, and gorgeous as a field of flowers, stood the Baluchis in their many-coloured garments and turbans; they filled the broad, deep bed of the ravine, they clustered on both banks, and covered the plain beyond. Guarding their heads with their large dark shields, they shook their sharp swords, beaming in the sun, their shouts rolling like a peal of thunder, as with frantic gestures they dashed forward with demoniac strength and ferocity full against the front of the 22nd. But with shouts as loud, and shrieks as wild and fierce as theirs, and hearts as big, and arms as strong, the Irish soldiers met them with the queen of weapons—the musket—and sent their foremost masses rolling back in blood."

The Baluchis closed their dense masses, and again the shouts, the rolling fire of musketry, and the dreadful rush of their swordsmen were heard and seen along the whole line; and such a fight ensued as has seldom been recorded in the annals of war. These wild warriors continually advanced, sword and shield in hand, striving in all the fierceness of their valour to break into the opposing ranks; no fire of small-arms, no thrust of bayonets, no swooping discharges of grape from the guns, which were planted in one fearful mass on the right, could drive the gallant soldiers back; they gave their breasts to be shot at, they leaped upon the guns by twenties at a time; their dead went down the slope by hundreds, but the gaps in their masses were continually filled up from the rear; the survivors of the front rank still pressed forward with unabated fury, and the bayonet and the sword clashed in full and frequent conflict.

Our loss in officers was heavy, and our native troops, deprived of leaders though not of gallantry, were several times forced into rearguard action; but at a given moment a charge made on the enemy's right by our entire but small body of horse, under the command of Colonel Pattle, won the day. The Baluchis had kept their ground for more than three hours, but now they began to retreat in masses, still keeping well together, with their broad shields slung over their backs and their heads half turned towards their pursuers. The victors followed closely, pouring in volley after volley, until tired of slaughtering. "Yet," says Napier, "those stern, implacable warriors preserved their habitual swinging stride, and would not quicken it to a run, though death was at their heels."

In this conflict our officers and men, together with our native troops, showed the greatest courage. The chief part of the battle was a hand-to-hand fight. "The noble soldier Pennefather," as Sir Charles Napier admiringly called him, fell on the top of the bank, to all appearance mortally wounded, and his place was instantly taken by Major Pool. Major Teesdale, followed by his sepoys, rode desperately over the ridge into the midst of the Baluchis, and was instantly killed by shot and sabre. Major Jackson followed the heroic example of Teesdale, and met the same fate. Two brave havildars kept close to them in advance of their regiment, and, like their leaders, they were also killed, but not until they had slain several of the fiercest of the enemy. Lieutenant M'Murdogh, of the General's staff, rode, like Teesdale and Jackson, into the very heart of the Baluchi mass; his horse was killed under him, yet he rose instantly, and meeting Jehan Mohabad, one of the most warlike of the chiefs, slew him in the midst of his clan. Then, while engaged with several in front, one came behind and struck at him, but a sergeant of the 22nd killed that enemy so instantly that his blow fell harmless.

M'Murdogh turned and did the same service for his preserver, cleaving the head of a Baluchi who was aiming at his back. Captain Jacob and Lieutenant Fitzgerald performed similar exploits. Six European officers and sixty sergeants and privates were killed, and fourteen officers and about 200 men wounded. The loss of the Baluchis was enormous; a careful computation gave it as 6,000—1,000 bodies were heaped in the ravine alone. What greater proof is wanting of the great courage and tenacity of the Baluchi warrior, who is now linking his glorious traditions with ours by deeds worthy of his ancient prowess?

THE FIRST SIKH WAR

(Moodkee, 1845)

It can hardly be said that when Sir H. Hardinge arrived in India in 1844 he found our frontier forces insufficient in numbers or unprepared for action. When the first Sikh War broke out in December, 1845, there were at Umballa 12,000 men with 32 guns, at Ferozepore 10,472 with 24 guns, and at Ludhiana 7,235 with 12 guns. Including the force of 1,800 at the hill stations this made a total of 32,479 men with 68 guns—a very respectable little British army.

On December 7th and 8th news came from Lahore to the effect that preparations were being made on a large scale for artillery, stores, and all the munitions of war, but as yet no infantry or artillery had been reported to have left Lahore, nor had a single Sikh soldier crossed the Sutlej. On the 9th, at night, Captain Nicholson, the assistant political agent at Ferozepore, reported that a portion of the Sikh army had approached within three miles of the river. On the 10th no intelligence was received from Lahore confirmatory of Captain Nicholson's report, and the opinion continued to prevail that the Sikh army would not cross the Sutlej. Our troops, however, moved on the 10th, 11th, 12th, in pursuance of orders given on the 7th and 8th; and the whole of the forces destined to move up to the Sutlej were in full march on the 12th. Some days later the whole of the Ludhiana force was moved up with the Umballa force, restricting the defence of Ludhiana to the fort, which could be securely garrisoned by the soldiers left at that post, unless attacked by heavy artillery, which was a very improbable contingency.

This fine body of men, by a rapid march on Busseean, an important point where the roads leading from Umballa and Kurnaul meet, formed the advanced column of the army, and secured the supplies which had been laid in at Busseean. Up to the morning of the 12th, the information from Lahore had not materially varied; but, by the reports received on that day, the general aspect of affairs appeared more warlike. Still no Sikh aggression had been committed, and no artillery had moved down to the river. On the 13th, however, Sir Henry Hardinge received precise information that the Sikh army had crossed the Sutlej, and was concentrating a great force on the left bank of the river. Sir Henry immediately ordered Brigadier Wheeler to march, with 4,500 men and twenty-one guns, early on the 14th from Ludhiana to Busseean, which place had been filled with provisions by arrangements made through Major Broadfoot with the native chiefs—provisions upon which the British army depended in its advance to Ferozepore. By the afternoon of the 14th, Brigadier Wheeler was in front of Busseean. The main column, under the Commander-in-Chief, from Umballa, did not reach Busseean until the 16th.

The Sikhs had not completed the passage of their heavy guns until the 16th, and, by the 17th, the advance of the force under the Commander-in-Chief began to tell upon them, for on the 17th the main body, consisting, according to the Sikh accounts, of 25,000 regulars and 88 guns, under Lal Singh, took possession of the wells around the village of Ferozeshah, whilst Tej Singh with 23,000 men and 67 guns remained opposite to Ferozepore. Now the only road by which an army can march from Busseean to Ferozepore (on account of the scarcity of water) passes through Moodkee, and is about twenty miles, Ferozeshah being mid-way. Knowing that the Commander-in-Chief must carry these works before he could relieve Ferozepore, the Sikhs commenced on December 17th to throw up entrenchments around the wells at Ferozeshah in order to stop the advance of the column under the Commander-in-Chief. Not knowing the strength of his column, and thinking it was only the advance guard of the British army, 12,000

Sikhs, chiefly cavalry, and 22 guns, under the command of Lal Singh, left the camp at Ferozeshah, early on the 18th, and had taken up their position at Moodkee before the arrival of the British army. No sooner had our troops arrived than a scout sent by the political agent brought the news that the enemy was only three miles away.

The British troops hastily got under arms and moved to their positions. Sir Hugh Gough immediately pushed forward the horse artillery and cavalry, and directed the infantry, accompanied by the field batteries, to move forward in support. Sir Hugh's own description is a good one. He says, "We had not proceeded beyond two miles when we found the enemy in position. To resist their attack, and to cover the formation of the infantry, I advanced the cavalry, under Brigadiers White, Gough, and Mactier, rapidly to the front in columns of squadrons, and occupied the plain. They were speedily followed by the five troops of horse artillery under Brigadier Brooke, who took up a forward position, having the cavalry then on his flank.

"The country is a dead flat, covered at short intervals with a low but in some places thick jhow jungle, and dotted with sandy hillocks. The enemy screened their infantry and artillery behind this jungle and such undulations as the ground afforded; and whilst our twelve battalions formed from echelon of brigade into line they opened a very severe cannonade upon our advancing troops, which was vigorously replied to by the battery of horse artillery under Brigadier Brooke, which was soon joined by the two light field batteries. The rapid and well-directed fire of our artillery appeared soon to paralyse that of the enemy; and as it was necessary to complete our infantry dispositions without advancing the artillery too near to the jungle, I directed the cavalry under Brigadiers White and Gough to make a flank movement on the enemy's left, with a view of threatening and turning that flank if possible. With praiseworthy gallantry, the 3rd Light Dragoons [now known as the 3rd (King's Own) Hussars], with the second brigade of cavalry, consisting of the Body-guard and 5th Light Cavalry, with a portion of the 4th Lancers,* turned the left of the Sikh army, and sweeping along the whole rear of its infantry and guns silenced for a time the latter and put their numerous cavalry to flight. Whilst this movement was taking place on the enemy's left, I directed the remainder of the 4th Lancers, the 9th Irregular Cavalry* under Brigadier Mactier, with a light field battery, to threaten their right.

"This manœuvre was also successful. Had not the infantry and guns of the enemy been

* Native regiments.

screened by the jungle, these brilliant charges of the cavalry would have been productive of greater effect.

"When the infantry advanced to the attack, Brigadier Brooke rapidly pushed on his horse artillery close to the jungle, and the cannonade was resumed on both sides. The infantry, under Major-Generals Sir Harry Smith, Gilbert, and Sir John M'Caskill, attacked in echelon of lines the enemy's infantry, almost invisible amongst wood and the approaching darkness of night. The opposition of the enemy was such as might have been expected from troops who had everything at stake, and who had long vaunted of being irresistible. Their ample and extended line, from their great superiority of numbers, far outflanked ours; but this was counteracted by the flank movements of our cavalry. The attack of the infantry now commenced, and the roll of fire from this powerful arm soon convinced the Sikh army that they had met with a foe they little expected; and their whole force was driven from position after position with great slaughter, and the loss of seventeen pieces of artillery, some of them of heavy calibre; our infantry using that never-failing weapon, the bayonet, whenever the enemy stood. Night only saved them from worse disaster, for this stout conflict was maintained during an hour and a half of dim starlight, amidst a cloud of dust from the sandy plain, which yet more obscured every object."

Our troops in this battle consisted of 3,850 Europeans and 8,500 natives, making a total of 12,350 rank and file, and 41 guns. Sixteen officers were killed and 200 men; forty-eight officers wounded and 609 men, of whom 153 died subsequently of their wounds, or were disabled. Amongst those who fell was the hero of Jellalabad, Sir Robert Sale; he had his left thigh shattered by grape-shot, and the wound proved mortal. Had there been more daylight, the rout of the enemy would have been more complete; as it was, seventeen of their guns out of twenty were captured, and their loss in killed and wounded was very severe. Yet it must be said that, in this battle of Moodkee, our friend the enemy fought bravely and well—so well that, casting a backward glance on that day of glorious deeds, we are now proud to claim him as a friend indeed.

ALIWAL AND SOBRAON

(1846)

BADLY beaten at Ferozeshah, the Sikhs naturally expected that the British troops would at once follow up their advantage by crossing the Sutlej and advancing on the capital; but in order to do this successfully it was necessary to wait the arrival of the powerful battering train now moving upwards with the Meerut force under Sir John Grey, consisting of the 9th Lancers, the 16th Lancers, and her Majesty's 10th and 53rd Regiments of Foot, with the 43rd and 59th Regiments of Native Infantry.

The Sikhs, mistaking this delay for irresolution, resolved to make another effort to maintain their position on the left bank of the Sutlej; and for this purpose they began to construct a new bridge of boats, not very far from the spot where they crossed the river after having been driven from Ferozeshah. Our Army of the Sutlej was stationed some distance from the river, and no opposition was offered by them. The bridge of boats was soon constructed, and works thrown up in front of it with much military skill, in a position very favourable to defence. The opposite banks were high, and the river, where the bridge was laid, made a slight curve inwards, so as to throw those banks sufficiently forward to afford protection to both flanks of the advanced position from heavy artillery placed in battery. Above the bridge, and not far from it, was a good ford, which facilitated the communications with the forces on the opposite bank. Advantage had also been taken of the slenderness of our troops at Ludhiana to effect a passage for a force of about 10,000 men of all arms, in the neighbourhood of that town. No attack was made either on the town or cantonment of Ludhiana; the object of this force appeared to be rather to entrench itself near the place at which it crossed, in order to obstruct our progress and to cut off the passage of supplies to Ferozepore, and to intercept the communication between the posts.

As soon as the Meerut force joined the Commander-in-Chief's camp, immediate measures were taken to reinforce the Ludhiana post and the station at Busseean. Some native infantry, some light cavalry, and some guns were sent thither, and the sick, the women, and the children were removed thence to Umballa. Meanwhile Sir Harry Smith had been detached to reduce Dhurmkote and keep open the communication for supplies and ammunition from our rear. Sir Harry was now reinforced, having with him 7,000 men and 24 guns, and it was confidently believed that he could at one and the same time relieve Ludhiana and protect the whole of our rear. Dhurmkote was evacuated at his approach. On the way from Jugraon to Ludhiana he lost a good deal of his baggage, and sustained some heavy fusilades, which he did not wait to return. His troops were much harassed when he reached Ludhiana, but his presence put an end to the consternation which was becoming general in that part of the country.

The Sirdar Runjur Singh had strongly entrenched himself at Aliwal, about eight miles to the westward of Ludhiana. He had 15,000 men and 56 guns, and on the evening of January 26th he received a reinforcement of 12 guns and 4,000 regular troops. Sir Harry Smith most gallantly attacked the Sikhs on January 28th with not more than 16,000 men in all. The right of the Sikh force rested on Bundree, and their left on Aliwal. When they had advanced a short distance from their entrenched camp, they cannonaded the British for half an hour, until our brave fellows stormed the village of Aliwal, the key of their position. The whole of the British line then began to advance. Her Majesty's 16th Lancers charged in the most gallant style, but the Sikhs lay down on the ground and the Lancers could not easily reach them. In this position the Sikhs did deadly work with their muskets and keen swords.

The 16th Lancers had upwards of a hundred men killed or wounded. The great mass of Sikh infantry could be broken only by our artillery. One Sikh cannon after another was captured. So ably were the orders of attack conducted, each column and line arriving at its point of attack to the very moment, that the enemy was soon driven headlong back over the river, and all their guns were captured or destroyed. Only one gun was carried by the Sikhs to the opposite bank, and there it was spiked by Lieutenant Holmes, of the Irregular Cavalry, and Gunner Scott, of the Horse Artillery, who forded the river in pursuit. The victory was complete, and great was the confusion among the Sikhs.

After this complete and decisive victory there was a breathing space in the campaign. The Sikhs at Sobraon went on strengthening their position, while Sir Hugh Gough waited for his artillery and reinforcements. From January 14th till the beginning of February the enemy was industriously employed in building defences, under the direction, it is said, of a Spanish engineer. The army under Sir Charles Napier, which had been assembled at Sukkar by order of the Governor-General, consisting of 16,000 men, was moving up to the left bank of the Sutlej towards Ferozepore, and would have proved, had the war lasted, a most valuable reinforcement to the Army of the Sutlej. It had by this time reached Bhawalpur, opposite Mooltan, and as the Nawab of that place had intimated to the British Government his intention of remaining neutral, the Governor-General, feeling that the blow must be struck and the contest decided at Lahore, requested Sir Charles Napier to come on with his staff in advance of his army, and to join him without delay, being desirous of having the assistance of that distinguished officer in the pending struggle. Sir Charles Napier did not, however, arrive in time to add to the glories of Sobraon, but the heavy guns from Delhi reached the Commander-in-Chief's camp on February 9th.

Although on the first intelligence of the battle of Aliwal, and at sight of the numerous bodies which floated from the neighbourhood of that battlefield down to the bridge of boats at Sobraon, the Sikhs seemed much shaken and disheartened, they now appeared to be as confident as ever of being able to defy us in their entrenched position and to prevent our passage of the river. The soldiers were chiefly those who had been trained by the French and Italian officers. They had strong walls, only to be surmounted by scaling ladders, which afforded a secure protection for triple lines of musketry. In all they were 34,000 men with 70 pieces of artillery; their position was united by a good bridge to a reserve of 20,000 men on the opposite bank, on which was a considerable camp and some artillery, commanding and flanking our field-works.

Sir Hugh Gough's forces consisted of 6,533 Europeans and 9,691 natives, making a total of 16,224 rank and file, with 99 guns. Sir Hugh ordered this force to march at half-past three, on the morning of Tuesday, February 10th, when his men would be fresh and there would be a certainty of many hours of daylight. The troops began to move out of camp at the very moment appointed, and they marched in silence to their destination. Sir Hugh was now strong in cavalry and very strong in artillery. He at once put his battering and disposable artillery in position in an extended semicircle, embracing within its fire the works of the Sikhs.

It had been intended that the cannonade should commence at daybreak, but so heavy a mist hung over the plain and river that it was necessary to wait. It was half-past six before the whole of the artillery was developed. Dr. Macgregor, in his "History of the Sikhs," gives a graphic description of the opening of the action. He says: "Nothing could have been conceived grander than the effect of the batteries when they opened, as the cannonade passed along from the Sutlej to Little Sobraon in one continued roar of guns and mortars; while, ever and anon, the rocket like a spirit of fire winged its rapid flight high above the batteries in its progress towards the Sikh entrenchments. Well might the Commander-in-Chief call the opening of the cannonade ' most spirited and well directed.' The Sikh guns responded with shot and shell, but neither appeared to do much execution; the latter were seen bursting in mid-air ere they reached the British batteries, while some of the shot passed over Rhodawala, and struck the ground in front of General Gilbert's division. It now became a grand artillery concert, and the infantry divisions and brigades looked on with a certain degree of interest, somewhat allied, however, to vexation, lest the artillery should have the whole work to themselves. The Commander-in-Chief, however, was determined to give full play to an arm which he had not possessed to an efficient extent in other hard-fought battles. It was reported that the guns were to play for four hours at least; but there is some reason to believe that the rapid firing had nearly exhausted the ammunition before half that time had elapsed, and it was once more to be proved that the British Infantry were not to remain mute spectators of a battle. ' Notwithstanding,' wrote the Commander-in-Chief, ' the formidable calibre of our guns, mortars, and howitzers, and the admirable way in which they were served, and aided by a rocket battery, it would have been visionary to expect that they could have silenced the fire of seventy pieces behind well-constructed batteries of earth, planks, and fascines, or dislodge troops covered either by redoubts or epaulements or within a treble line of trenches.' "

The utmost ingenuity of the Sikhs and their European advisers had been exerted to render the works at Sobraon vastly superior to those at Ferozeshah. They had aimed at absolute impregnability, and a French officer assured Tej Singh that it was utterly impossible for the British to make good their entrance. But it may be said they reckoned without the small host opposing them. The British were now about to try with the musket and the bayonet. At nine o'clock, Brigadier Stacey's brigade, supported on either flank by Captain Horford's and Fordyce's batteries, and Lieutenant-Colonel Lane's troop of horse artillery, moved to the attack in admirable order. The infantry and guns aided each other correlatively. The former marched steadily on in line, which they halted only to correct when necessary, while the latter took up successive positions at the gallop, until at length they were within three hundred yards of the heavy batteries of the Sikhs. But notwithstanding the regularity and coolness, and the scientific character of the assault, which Brigadier Wilkinson well supported, so hot was the fire of cannon and musketry kept up by the Khalsa troops that it seemed for some moments impossible that the entrenchments could be won under it. This fire was all the more formidable from the fact that the Sikhs employed zumburuks—guns mounted on camels and carrying pound shot.

There was a temporary check or pause, but, soon, persevering gallantry triumphed, and the whole army had the satisfaction of seeing Brigadier Stacey's gallant soldiers driving the Sikhs in confusion before them within the area of their encampment. Every impediment was cleared, the entrenchments were passed, and our matchless infantry stood erect and compact within the Sikh camp. Said the Commander-in-Chief: "Her Majesty's 10th, 53rd, and 80th Regiments, with the 33rd, 43rd, 59th, and 63rd Native Infantry, moving at a firm and steady pace, never fired a shot until they had passed the barriers opposed to them—a forbearance much to be commended, and most worthy of constant imitation, to which may be attributed the success of their first effort, and the small loss they sustained."

This attack was crowned with all the success it deserved, and, led by its gallant Commander, Major-General Sir Robert Dick, obtained the admiration of the army, which witnessed its disciplined valour. When checked by the formidable obstacles and superior numbers to which the attacking division was opposed, the second division, under Major-General Gilbert, afforded the most opportune assistance by rapidly advancing to the attack of the enemy's batteries, entering their fortified position after a severe struggle, and sweeping through the interior of the camp. This division inflicted a very severe loss on the retreating enemy. Together with a portion of Gilbert's division, the troops advanced immediately the order was received. But, if intended to support Stacey on the right of the enemy's position, they missed the object, for they unfortunately came in front of the centre and strongest portion of the encampment, unsupported either by artillery or cavalry. Her Majesty's 29th and 1st European Light Infantry, with undaunted bravery, rushed forward, crossed a dry nullah and found themselves exposed to one of the hottest fires of musketry that can possibly be imagined; and what rendered it still more galling was that the Sikhs were themselves concealed behind high walls, over which the European soldiers could not climb. To remain under such a fire without the power of returning it with any effect would have been madness—the men would have been annihilated. Thrice did Her Majesty's 29th Regiment charge the works, and thrice were they obliged to retire, each time followed by the Sikhs, who spared none. Similar was the fate of the 1st European Light Infantry, who, in retiring, had their ranks thinned by musketry and their wounded men and officers cut up by the Sikhs. To the latter, the nullah afforded an admirable defence, for the slope was in their favour, while the Europeans on the high bank were completely exposed. At length the second division, which at Ferozeshah had driven the Sikhs before them, capturing their guns at the point of the bayonet and entering their encampment, were led to the right of the entrenchment at Sobraon. The second division was followed by the first division, which, under Sir Harry Smith, dashed against the enemy's left. Yet it was not until the 3rd Light Dragoons, under Major-General Sir Joseph Thackwell, had moved forward and ridden through the openings of the entrenchments in single file, re-forming as they passed them, and galloped over and cut down the obstinate defenders of batteries and field-works—indeed, it was not until the weight of three entire divisions of infantry, with every field-artillery gun which could be sent to their aid, had been cast into the scale—that victory finally fell to our troops. The fire of the Sikhs slackened, then almost ceased; and the victors, pressing them on every side, swept them in masses over the bridge of boats and into the Sutlej, which a sudden rise of seven inches had rendered scarcely fordable.

In their efforts to reach the right bank through the deepened water, they suffered a terrible

WITH THE EXPEDITIONARY FORCE, 1914.

carnage from our horse artillery. Hundreds fell under this cannonade; hundreds upon hundreds were drowned in attempting the perilous passage.

Thus terminated, in the brief space of two hours, this most remarkable conflict, in which the military combinations of the Commander-in-Chief were fully and ably carried into effect. The enemy's select regiments of regular infantry had been dispersed, and a large proportion destroyed, with the loss, since the campaign began, of 220 pieces of artillery taken in action. Over sixty-seven guns, together with upwards of 200 camel-swivels, and numerous standards were captured within the entrenchments. Before the hour of noon this great battle was over. It might, indeed, be well termed a glorious fight and complete in its results. The battles of Moodkee, Ferozeshah, and Aliwal had weakened the power of the Sikhs, but the battle of Sobraon had completely broken it. It was, of course, bought at a dear price. Her Majesty's 29th Regiment alone lost in killed and wounded thirteen officers, eight sergeants, and 157 rank and file. The loss of the 1st European Light Infantry was still heavier. Her Majesty's 31st, which had fought most nobly at Moodkee, Ferozeshah, and Aliwal, had seven officers and 147 rank and file killed and wounded at Sobraon. Her Majesty's 50th, or Queen's Own, had twelve officers and 227 rank and file killed and wounded.

Her Majesty's 10th Foot lost three officers, three sergeants, and 127 rank and file. These regiments suffered the most, but others suffered severely. The total loss was 320 killed, 2,063 wounded. The brave Sir Robert Dick, who led the attack on the entrenchments, received a mortal wound after he had entered them. Says the historian: "Thus fell, most gloriously, at the moment of victory, this veteran officer, displaying the same energy and intrepidity as when, thirty-five years ago in Spain, he was the distinguished leader of the 42nd Highlanders" (the 1st Battalion of the Black Watch).

Fearful had been the loss of the Sikhs. Five days after the action, and when the walls of the entrenchments had been nearly levelled with the ground, the sandbank in the middle of the river was completely covered with their dead bodies, and the ground within their encampment thickly strewn with carcasses of men and horses.

Before daylight the next morning six regiments of native infantry and six guns had, by means of country boats, crossed the Sutlej at a point nearer to the capital than where the débris of the Sikh army was stationed. On the following day the bridge of boats was nearly completed by the able and indefatigable Major Abbott, of the Engineers. Had the British then followed up the Sikhs they might have made their way without resistance to Lahore, and have there renewed the conflict; but such was not the intention of our commanders, and the capital of the Punjab was destined to be occupied by the British without any repetition of the life-consuming struggles which had occurred on the left bank of the Sutlej. If pressed, they would have fought hard in their despair; but the power of the Sikhs was in reality destroyed. Sham Singh, Dhubal Singh, Hera Singh, Kishen Singh, Mobaruck Ali, Newaz Khan —all their bravest sirdars and leaders had perished. The discomfited warriors who survived, being left to themselves, began to disperse. Our army quietly crossed the river, and took undisputed possession of Kussoor, which, in former times, had twice defied the power of Runjeet Singh. On February 14th the Governor-General announced by proclamation, dated from Kussoor, that the British army had crossed the Sutlej and entered the Punjab, "in accordance with the intentions expressed in the proclamation of December 13th last, as having been forced upon him for the purpose of effectually protecting the British provinces, and vindicating the authority of the British Government, and punishing the violators of treaties and the disturbers of the public peace."

The Government of Lahore paid, as an indemnity for the expense of the war, about one million sterling. The Jullunder Doab, the district between the Beas and Sutlej, was confiscated and proclaimed British territory. All the guns we had taken were to be retained, and all those which the Sikhs had ever directed against the British were to be given up, and the Sikh army was to dismiss and break up for ever and a day.

This Punjab war is remarkable for the fact that it was the cheapest and shortest ever waged. It cost the British Government about £2,000,000, and lasted only sixty days. An indemnity of £1,500,000 from the Lahore Durbar and Ghoolab Singh resulted, with a net annual revenue from confiscated territory of £500,000. But these things could never be so valuable to us as the whole-hearted loyalty and bravery of the gallant Sikh himself, who to-day fights as nobly and fiercely by our side as in the old "forties" he strove against us. And if in those days, to our cost as well as our admiration, we learned the meaning of the "Pride of the Punjab," we shall soon be able to appreciate it from a different standpoint.

THE STORMING OF THE TAKU FORTS

(1859)

THE trouble arose between the allied French and British and the Chinese over Tien-tsin, the port of Pekin. On June 25th, 1859, Admiral Hope attempted to force the entrance of the Pei-ho River at the Taku Forts with a few gunboats, but his endeavours were frustrated. In the following year allied forces of British and French troops, under General Sir Hope Grant and General de Montauban, were landed at Peh-tang, some eight miles north of Taku, while the allied fleets safeguarded their movement by watching the mouth of the river. These troops marched inland to avoid the marshes intervening between Peh-tang and Taku, and joined battle with the Chinese Field Army, defeating them at Sin-hid on August 12th. Two days later they descended the north bank of the Pei-ho and seized the town of Tang-ku, three miles north of the forts.

The Taku Forts were four in number, and the question arose between the two generals as to the best method of attack. Sir Hope Grant was in favour of beginning with the smallest fort, but de Montauban maintained it would be better to cross the river and attack the largest fort in the south first. After some friction the former course was adopted, but Montauban was so little in favour of it that he sent only a few hundred men and attended the battle himself merely as a spectator, and without his sword. But this unfortunate little difference was soon forgotten in the deadly work of the day. Many brave deeds were done; the most furious conflict took place when the storming party reached the fort and were crowded together between the inner ditch and the ramparts. Here they were safe from the Chinese musketry, but they immediately became a target for big stones, cannon balls, and stifling stinkpots which the Chinese dropped on their heads. Again and again the scaling ladders were planted against the ramparts, where the Chinese caught them and either pulled them up into the fort or hurled them down, shooting or spearing all who gained a footing within reach of their weapons. The officers and men tried to force entries where the artillery had broken down the embrasures for the guns. A gallant Frenchman sprang on to the ramparts, clubbed a Chinaman with his rifle, snatched another which was handed up to him, fired, and immediately fell speared through the head. Another with a pickaxe gained the top of the wall and tried to break it down; the brave fellow was immediately shot dead, but Lieut. Burslem, who was behind him, seized the pickaxe and continued the work. With many another heroic deed of this kind the fort was eventually captured, the Chinese capitulating after very heavy losses. Our Indian troops behaved with the greatest gallantry in this momentous struggle.

THE THIRD AFGHAN WAR

(1880)

WHEN Yakoub Khan learned that Sir Louis Cavagnari had been sent on a mission to Kabul, his grief and repentance over his terrible outrages seemed beyond expression. He protested too much, and nobody believed him; indeed, before the mission had set out, there had been quite sufficient incentive for the British Government to teach the native authorities at Kabul a severe lesson. When the truth of the matter was felt, rather than known, three columns were despatched to the seat of trouble. The most important of these, which proceeded by the Kurram Road, was led by General Roberts. Its composition was as follows:—Two batteries Horse and Field Artillery; one Mountain Train battery; one squadron 9th Lancers; 67th South Hampshire Regiment; 72nd (Duke of Albany's Own) Highlanders; 92nd (Gordon) Highlanders; 12th and 14th Bengal Cavalry; 5th Gurkhas and a wing of the 5th Punjab; 23rd Pioneers; 5th and 28th Punjab Infantry; 3rd Sikhs, and one company of sappers and miners, making a total of barely 8,000 men.

So determined was the spirit of these men that, as battle followed battle on the way to the capital, Yakoub Khan, with twenty-five principal citizens of Kabul, eventually surrendered. It was probably a subterfuge on the part of the Amir to say that he no longer had any power over his people. At all events, he was kept in durance vile, and next day General Roberts advanced on Kabul. Then followed the battle of Charasiah.

Charasiah is twelve miles distant from Kabul, and its name signifies "Four Water-mills." Here the tired troops camped, while cavalry patrols were sent out to scour the vicinity. Like the Saxons on the eve of the Battle of Hastings, our men little thought that the dawn would bring a decisive battle; but, unlike the Saxons on that occasion, though exhausted, they were always ready for any emergency that the morrow might bring. In evidence of this, two cavalry patrols pushed forward along the ways that led to Kabul before the first light of dawn. The northern road was taken by a party of twenty men of the 14th Bengal Lancers, under Captain Neville, while twenty of the 9th Lancers, under Captain Apperley, took the southern road. Three hours later, as Captain Neville's party was passing through a village, one of his men had his horse shot under him. At the same time, Apperley, in another village, was being hard pressed by the enemy. Major Mitford, with twenty Lancers, was immediately sent to his relief, while a band of native infantry was despatched in all haste to succour Neville. Following immediately on these operations came news that the enemy was advancing in great force from Kabul. They were focussing on the passes of the northern hills. It then became an immediate matter of British tactics to forestall or dislodge them. The event proved that they had to be dislodged, and in this matter there was severe and prolonged fighting before they were driven back. Ultimately the enemy fled incontinently towards Kabul.

Some incidents of this battle are worth recording. It was here that Major (afterwards Field-Marshal Sir George) Stuart White won his Victoria Cross, while commanding the 92nd Highlanders. For a long time he pounded the enemy with artillery, and raked him with rifle fire, but all in vain; he could not dislodge the obstinate foe. The most decisive method was to storm the hill, with a view to the ultimate efficiency of cold steel.

Says the *Gazette*: "Advancing with two companies of his regiment, he came upon a body of the enemy, strongly posted, and outnumbering his force by eighteen to one. His men being exhausted, and immediate action necessary, Major White took a rifle, and, going on by himself, shot dead the leader of the enemy."

And this was where the Afghans were at a disadvantage. The loss of their leader meant everything to them, for they were not as our soldiers—every man a leader if emergency requires. They began to fall back on the further slope of the hill, fearing the onslaught of the Highlanders, who were on top of it, victorious. It is extraordinary that in this important engagement our losses up to this point were nothing more than three Highlanders killed and six wounded, one cavalry soldier killed and three wounded.

While this engagement was proceeding, General Baker was leading his 72nd Highlanders across the hills, with a following of No. 2 Mounted Battery, some Gatling guns, and the wings of the 5th Gurkhas, 5th Punjab Infantry, and 23rd Pioneers. They fought their way over precipitous ground, and through 4,000 of the enemy. The resistance they met with remains to this day as a proof of the fighting powers of our then enemy. After two hours' stubborn fighting, regulated by the able generalship of Baker, the hill was at last taken in the rear by a flanking movement of the Gordons. It was a scene to live in the memory, when the gallant 92nd, cheered on by Cameron's pipes, stormed the hill. The dash and vigour of the assault no doubt carried the position, but the moral effect of Cameron and his pipes, to say nothing of brave colours flying, had to be reckoned with.

From this point the march on Kabul was unimpeded. When General Roberts arrived he found the place abandoned by the enemy. But there still remained some Afghans entrenched on a high hill to the rear of Bala Hissar, in such a position that it was necessary to dislodge them before entering the city, especially as behind them the enemy was in great force on the Ridge of Asmai. There was very severe fighting over the dislodgment of these Afghans, but on the fourth day General Roberts had removed every obstruction to his entry into Kabul. It was a great moment when he hoisted our Standard on the walls of Kabul.

TEL-EL-KEBIR AND KASSASSIN

(1882)

THE British campaign arose out of the rebellious ambition of Arabi Pasha. The culminating point of the campaign was the battle of Tel-el-Kebir—the word signifying "A large village." Arabi Pasha was of common origin, having risen from the ranks of the Viceroy's army to the position of a somewhat famous colonel. His motto was "Egypt for the Egyptians." In this he left out of account the fact that Britain had tremendous interests in Egypt, including £4,000,000 of Suez Canal stock. Blinding himself also to the fact that Britain could not afford to lose the direct route to India, Arabi Pasha continued to oppose the growth of British influence even up to the point that he wished to rule Egypt himself.

The free expression of this ambition led to the bombardment of Alexandria and the destruction of Arabi's forts. Being defeated, his hatred of British influence grew stronger than ever. He retired into the interior and began mobilising his countrymen. As soon as this was known, it became necessary to send out a British army to hunt out the rebellious Arabi and put an end to his ambitions for ever. This army, under the command of Sir Garnet (afterwards Viscount) Wolseley, comprised 40,000 men, and was derived from India, Malta, Cyprus and Gibraltar.

This force landed at a port on the Canal and pressed on towards Kassassin. The rebels attempted to check its progress at Mahuta, but they were easily driven off. Very soon afterwards General Graham, with his vanguard, arrived at Kassassin, where he entrenched himself in obedience to a strict order to hold it at all costs. Many attacks were made, but they were all successfully foiled There were two considerable engagements contested here, but they were merely preliminaries to that at Tel-el-Kebir, which was of the greatest moment. The 13th Bengal Lancers were engaged on the occasion when the Egyptians made a second attack at Kassassin. Then they were moved up to Tel-el-Kebir.

The fortified defences of Tel-el-Kebir were very strong. The British were in position before the first streak of dawn, and everything was "all Sir Garnet," as Tommy Atkins has constantly said ever since. There was silence as the soldiers lay waiting for the word to advance, and, when at last it was given in a subdued tone, all arose and marched forward, and their footfalls on the soft sand were almost as noiseless as footfalls on the snow. Of this mysterious nocturnal advance in the silence of a mysterious land, a historian says: "The darkness around and above, with the stars shining down as they had done in the time of Pharaoh and the other dynasties of Egyptian kings lying entombed in the Pyramids . . . weird and ghostly was the effect of the dim streaks, looking like shadows of moving clouds, but which were really lines of men stealing over the desert."

The first indication that our approach was discovered came in the form of some scattered shots fired by the enemy's sentries; then came a bugle call from within the enemy's lines. This filled our men with enthusiasm, for it meant that the action would begin in the darkness, which was to our advantage. For a few minutes they marched on stealthily, then the whole line of the enemy's entrenchments, which had been unknown to us, was now clearly revealed by the sudden blaze of rifle fire. The simultaneous flash was so great that it lit up the whole scene. Immediately the British bugles sounded the charge, and our men on the instant sprang forward with loud cheers, then advanced rapidly but steadily on the foe.

The terrible conflict which ensued soon became general, and the infantry, once in close grips with the Egyptians, inflicted severe loss with the bayonet. It was to this astonishing "infantry" that the credit of victory was mainly due; the artillery and cavalry, together with a fine force of marines, were responsible for the infliction of heavy punishment on the foe in the confusion of their retreat.

In this battle the 20th Duke of Cambridge's Own Light Infantry ("Brownlow's Punjabis") fought with great bravery, and, by their heroic deeds, added "Tel el-Kebir" to the list of their battle honours.

During the course of the Egyptian campaign two other Indian regiments of cavalry, besides the 13th Bengal Lancers, and two of infantry besides the 20th, fought bravely, and all bear the "honours" of "Egypt 1882" and "Tel-el-Kebir." The 2nd Queen Victoria's Own Sappers and Miners (a native corps) also bear these "honours," in addition to "Suakin 1885" and "Tofrek."

BATTLES AROUND SUAKIN

El-Teb } 1884 Hasheen } 1885
Tamai } Tofrek }

EVERYWHERE throughout the Sudan the Mahdi, or False Prophet, had waged a successful rebellion against the authority of the Egyptian Government, which, since the crushing defeat of Arabi Pasha at Tel-el-Kebir, had fallen under Britain's protection. In order to bring this truculent disturber to submission it was necessary to send a British army to the relief of Tokar near Suakin. The Sudan had for a long time been the impenetrable stronghold of the slave trade. "If any part of God's earth was dyed with human blood," said Lord Wolseley, "it was this," and now in addition to this there was the memory of the treachery at El-Obeid, the capital of Kordofan, where Hicks Pasha's army was treacherously led into ambush and ultimately massacred. The Mahdi was not present in this battle, but he came later to see the body of Hicks, who was the last to die, and thrust his spear through the Pasha's body as an example to be followed by all his sheikhs. All this blood—more than the blood of slaves—cried out for vengeance.

As the rebellion spread eastward, Osman the Ugly hastened thither and further inflamed it. This man was a slave trader, whose chief grievance was that he had been ruined by the prohibition of the vile traffic. For a time he had a victorious career, completely annihilating force after force of Egyptian troops. During his investment of Sinkat and Tokar, Baker Pasha was despatched with a force of 3,600 men to the relief of those two towns. But here another terrible slaughter of the Egyptian troops took place in the battle—or rather, the massacre—of El-Teb. An eye witness says of this: "Inside the square the state of affairs was almost indescribable. Cavalry, infantry, mules, camels, falling baggage and dying men were crushed into a struggling, surging mass. The Egyptians were shrieking madly, hardly attempting to run away, but trying to shelter themselves one behind another."

"The conduct of the Egyptians was simply disgraceful," said another English officer; "armed with rifle and bayonet, they allowed themselves to be slaughtered without an effort at self-defence, by savages inferior in numbers and armed only with spears and swords."

Seeing the uselessness of attempting to rally such material, Baker, with his staff, put spurs to his horse and charged the enemy. This small band of determined men cut their way through the formidable array of swords and lances. Soon after this the defenders of Sinkat, finding their stores almost exhausted, decided to fight their way out. Accordingly, 400 men, with many women and children, set out from the town. The men fought valiantly, but they were overpowered by numbers, and only six men and thirty women were left to tell the horrible tale of butchery.

Meanwhile Tokar was still under siege, and Sir Gerald Graham was sent with a small force to relieve it. At El-Teb he came in contact with the Mahdi's forces; this time the victory was on our side. Having crushed the Mahdi for the time being, he set out for Suakin, which was the concentration point of the Government in its now extensive preparations to humble Osman Digna. They had called on the rebel chiefs to lay down their arms, but the call had met with a most defiant reply. Sir Gerald advanced on Tamai and bivouacked within a mile of the enemy's position. All night long the British were harassed by shot and shell, but victory came in the morning, though with regrettable loss of life. It was none the less crushing, however, and was followed by a temporary cessation of hostilities. It was not until the following spring that Osman Digna had recuperated sufficiently to face the British troops again. In the campaign which followed, his hordes were successful until after the battles of Hasheen and Tofrek.

It was early in the morning that General Graham with less than 1,000 men arrived at the foot of the hills to the east of Hasheen. He established himself with his staff on one of the hills, and from that point directed the battle which ensued. The wells of Hasheen lay below in the valley.

With the light of day the whole place was seen to be alive with riflemen. Says an eye-witness: "They crowded on the Hasheen hill; they swarmed through the underwood, and nothing could be seen but little puffs of smoke rising over the trees. Here and there a shriek, a groan, a gap in the ranks, instantly filled up, showed that some of the enemy's bullets had found a billet. But for one that hit, a thousand whistled harmlessly over us." Volley answered volley from both sides, and the bullets began to fall thick and fast. Where the Sikhs were engaged the fire was especially furious. The enemy showed considerable bravery, but after a while the distant fire of our troops proved too hot for them. Two squadrons of the Bengal Lancers, making a gallant show with their turbans, streaming pennants, and flashing spears, were launched against them, and some desperate fighting now took place in this part of the field. One of the squadrons was dismounted for the purpose of firing volleys, but, being taken at a disadvantage, was driven back with the loss of nine men. The Arabs were led on to the attack by an old sheikh mounted on a camel. He waved his spear frantically, and his equally fanatical followers rushed round the Bengalese flank to their rear. One Lancer officer—an Englishman—was seen to hew down two Arabs in quick succession ; while the life of another officer was only saved by the steel breastplate underneath his tunic, which before his departure his wife had insisted on his wearing. On the right, too, about the same time, a similar charge was made by the other two squadrons of Bengal Cavalry and the 5th Lancers. This rapid movement completely checked and scattered a large body of the enemy who were advancing down the Hasheen valley with the intention of turning the British flank. The swarthy-faced Indian troops, with their eyes flashing friendly rivalry beneath their turbans, vied with their fresh-complexioned British comrades to carry off the chief honours of that charge ; and so strong was this admirable rivalry that history can only say "Honours easy."

In the action at Tofrek the Indian Brigade were engaged and showed striking gallantry. The 17th Bengal Native Infantry (the Loyal Regiment) gave some ground at a very important moment, but it was against fearful odds. No more need be said than that "Tofrek" is among their battle honours.

Orders were given to Generals McNeill and Hudson to advance to a certain spot and construct three zarebas at a distance of from six to eight miles from Suakin. Here, at Tofrek, they suddenly found the enemy upon them. In the conflict which ensued, the main brunt of the assault fell upon the 15th Sikhs and the 28th Bombay Native Infantry. Time after time they received assaults with heavy fire, firmly standing their ground and maintaining an intact line. The battle raged most furiously round the Sikhs, a fact which was afterwards confirmed by the hundreds of dead Arabs which lay in front of their position. The Bombay Regiment, though not in the thick of the fight, fought bravely, as proved by the toll of the enemy's dead and wounded.

THE FRONTIER FIGHTING OF 1886

IN the frontier fighting (1886) against the Afghans and Tibetans many important events occurred. Those of greatest interest were the survey by the Afghan Boundary Commission, under Colonel Sir West Ridgeway; General Sir G. White's march with his Flying Column to the Zhob Valley; the Manipur Massacre; the attack by tribesmen on the Fort of Chilas, and the Wazaris' fierce assault on the troops encamped at Wano.

The Afghan Boundary Commission, which had returned to India in 1886, after a two years' survey in the wild country to the north, was commanded by Colonel Sir West Ridgeway. Among his troops was a detachment of the 11th Bengal Lancers and 20th Punjab Infantry, who, to quote the Official Gazette, "have upheld throughout by discipline, endurance, and good conduct the credit of Her Majesty's Army."

The work before them was difficult and dangerous, but the British officers and native soldiers carried it to a successful issue with unflagging cheerfulness and invincible courage.

Sir G. White's march into the Zhob Valley may

be described in terms of equal praise. The Flying Column marched rapidly through the valley, and reached Thanispa on October 15th. From that point they hurried on, meeting with little opposition, and finally took possession of the entire country, bringing the chiefs to terms, and binding them over to cease the predatory raids which had been the occasion of all the trouble.

The Manipur Massacre, a terrible affair, arose, four years later, through the ambitions of a would-be usurper. In this case it was the ruler's own brother who caused the trouble. On September 22nd, 1890, at two o'clock in the morning, the Residency in Manipur was startled by the sound of musketry. Then, while the inmates were preparing for the worst, the Maharajah himself came running, in a state of panic, and told Mr. Grimwood, the Agent, that his brother had attacked the palace, and that, as he had given up all hopes of retaining power, his only course was to abdicate in favour of the usurper.

The Maharajah was allowed to escape from the country, but no sooner did he find himself beyond the reach of his brother's strong arm than he made up his mind to return. After having weighed the whole facts of the case, the Government decided that the usurper was the better man, and therefore they took steps to keep the Maharajah at a distance, and to expel the Senapatti, whose ambitions and ideals were not for the good of Manipur.

In accordance with instructions, Mr. Quinton, Chief Commissioner in Assam, set out for Manipur to further the intentions of the Government. His force consisted of 400 Rifles of the 42nd and 44th Gurkha Regiments, which were deemed sufficient reinforcement to the 100 Rifles of the 43rd Gurkhas already at Manipur. This little band of 400 arrived at Manipur on March 22nd, and, after consultation, it was decided to call a *darbar*, so as to declare and ventilate the decision of the Government. It was in the back of the Government's mind to effect the arrest of the Senapatti. But he had evidently got to know this; at all events, neither he nor his followers attended the *darbar*.

Notwithstanding Mr. Grimwood's intervention, in which he explained to the usurper that the Government was favourable to him, nothing satisfactory could be brought about with either side. The fact was that the usurper, as well as the Senapatti, was entirely antagonistic to the aims of the British; consequently, the *darbar* was a complete failure.

There was no time to be wasted, and there was no time to speculate on what was "on the other side of the hill." At daybreak on the 24th, Colonel Skene, with 250 men, called at the palace to arrest the missing chief. The Manipurs had foreseen this. They were well prepared. They had 6,000 men and two guns as a welcome, and, though the gallant 250 put up a tremendous fight, they were ultimately forced back to the Residency. Swift after them came the enemy with their guns. A fierce siege of the Residency then followed. Towards evening there was a lull, and an armistice was agreed upon. But the natives, not knowing at that time the far-reaching failure of Punic, or Prussian, faith, played false. Mr. Quinton, Colonel Skene, Mr. Grimwood, Lieutenant Simpson of the 43rd Gurkhas, and Mr. Cossins, Assistant Secretary of the Chief Commissioner, were made prisoners by treachery, and then the guns belched forth again on the Residency. In the morning the little garrison was forced to retreat, and they took the road towards Cochar, their way being lighted by burning villages on every hand, while far in the rear the Residency itself proclaimed the temporary triumph of the natives. In this retreat was Mrs. Grimwood, whose record of her remarkable escape will be remembered.

It was a retreat, not a rout. The brave fighters of the greatest rearguard action in history, in the present war, may well call to mind that rear-guard action on a small scale, when our troops were, so to speak, pursued by defeat, fighting against it all the way. At last they fell in with Captain Cowley, in command of a small band,

and, joining forces with him, they made their way to Lakhpur.

Meanwhile, General Graham, with half a battalion of the King's Royal Rifles, No. 2 Mountain Battery R.A.; two battalions 4th Gurkhas and 12th Madras Infantry, and two guns, set out from Burma to the rescue of the battered but not beaten troops. General Collett, commanding a column, also made in all haste for Lakhpur. On the arrival of these two contingents the city was speedily taken. But—and here is the pity—before they could get to Manipur, the officers above mentioned, treacherously taken, were treacherously massacred.

THE RELIEF OF CHITRAL

(1895)

In the relief of Chitral a number of native regiments took part. In the spring of 1895 Britain was suddenly called to attention by the news, flashed along the cables, that hell had broken loose in Chitral. This probably meant that a few British officers, with a small band of Sikhs and other native troops, were in a most dangerous position in the capital of that state. The probability soon became a certainty, and great alarm was felt as to their safety. The next piece of bad news was that the British were hemmed up in a small fort, and, in that desperate position, were defending it against fearful odds, beating off wild hordes of tribesmen, and fighting, in grim despair, against the clock, hoping that time might bring succour and relief. And the jeopardy of this situation was not lessened by the fresh news that two little sections of the British army from Gilgit had to scale mountains more rugged than the Alps before penetrating into the lowlands of Chitral to the relief of the little garrison.

The Relief of Chitral

After news of an engagement on March 7th no tidings were received from Chitral Fort. Meanwhile came the official report of the defeat of Captain Goss at Mastuj, he and fifty-six men having been killed—fifty-six out of a total of seventy-one. This, with the death-like silence of Chitral, was appalling; and immediately Major-General Sir Robert Low was ordered to mobilise on the frontier of the enemy's territory, and Colonel Kelly, commanding the 32nd Pioneers in the Gilgit district, was given *carte blanche* to plan the relief of Chitral in whatever way might seem best to him.

The journey from Gilgit to Chitral is a stupendous undertaking for an army. The distance is 220 miles, and the way lies over a gigantic range of mountains containing passes deep with perpetual snow. When it became known that Colonel Kelly had actually undertaken this journey in the hope of reaching Chitral in time to render assistance to the beleaguered British, the heart of Britain was contracted. There was a chill fear abroad, and the despairing word "impossible" was in constant use. In the clubs men who knew those mountains gazed into each other's eyes and borrowed what hope they could. The apparently impossible had often been attempted before, and proved possible; so the nation waited, nursing that fire of courage which is always kept burning in its breast.

Low's force was as follows :—

1st Brigade (General Kinloch).—Royal Rifles, Bedfordshires, 1st Sikhs, 37th Dogras.

2nd Brigade (General Waterfield).—Gordons, Scottish Highlanders, 4th Sikhs, Guides' Infantry, Field Hospital.

3rd Brigade (General Gatacre).—Seaforth Highlanders, Buffs, 25th Punjabis, 4th Gurkhas, Field Hospital.

Divisional Troops.—Guides' Infantry, 11th Bengal Lancers, 13th Bengal Infantry, 23rd Pioneers, Bengal Sappers, East Lancashire Regiment, 29th and 30th Punjabis, Field Hospital.

Colonel Kelly's force consisted of two parties :—

(1) 200 Pioneers, 2 mountain guns, 40 Kashmir sappers, with 100 Hunzanagur levies.

(2) 100 Kashmir troops, under Lieut. Gough.

Low forced Malakand Pass. The enemy's strength was on the left side of the pass. Low brought his artillery to bear on this position, while the 4th Sikhs and Guides were thrown forward to scale the hills and carry the breastworks of loose stones; after which they were to work along the ridges and turn the enemy's flank.

No sooner had they come within range than the hillmen poured a fierce fire into their ranks;

but our men could not reply, as their stern business was to climb, and climb as quickly as possible. And a most desperate ascent it was, for they had to contend against not only a hail of bullets, but an avalanche of boulders as well. The officers suffered heavily, from the simple fact that they could easily be distinguished by their helmets among the turbaned troops.

It was a long and tragic climb, but at last it came to the point of the bayonet on the crest of the hill, and after more than three hours' fighting the defenders abandoned the position. The Sikhs and Guides, who carried this important point, had been nineteen hours under arms.

During this time the Scottish Borderers and the Gordons had forced their way up the centre of the pass until they now came to the last climb, which was the steepest of all. But it was their own native task that was before them, and, point by point, they scrambled upwards, helping each other up, and never flinching under the constant storm of lead. Seeing the desperate nature of their situation, Low despatched Kinloch's infantry to their support: the King's Royal Rifles on the left and the Bedfordshires and Dogras on the right; the 15th Sikhs being held in reserve. The Borderers and the Gordons not only held, but gained ground, and the Bedfordshires, when they came up, pushed right through the fighting line, and, supported by the Dogras, finished the fight the Borderers and the Gordons had so long contested. Clear over the ridge they drove the hillmen, and the Dogras never ceased pursuit of the routed foe until the survivors were dispersed in the Swat valley.

Kelly encountered much severe fighting on his difficult journey, and his daring and successful mission of relief can never be forgotten. The principal engagement, however, was at Malakand Pass, where, though victorious, Sir Robert Low's small force lost seventy killed and wounded.

Besides the many native regiments which took part in the relief of Chitral, special honour is due to the 14th (King George's Own) Ferozepore Sikhs, who were prominent in its defence. Their bravery of despair and their heroic patience in that defence have bequeathed to them a heritage of glory in the annals of Britain; and

> "The gold of glory, put to use,
> More glory doth beget."

BATTLE OF DARGAI

(1897)

The storming of the Dargai Heights was the most daring enterprise of the Tirah Expedition. In the middle of October, after much delay in the setting out, and just in time to meet the worst of the early winter storms, the Expedition duly reached its first camping-place beneath the ridge of Dargai. This was the initial obstacle to its advance into the Rakzai country. In order to clear this ridge, Sir William Lockhart sent forward the second division of his force, under General Yeatman-Biggs, which engaged the enemy in a desperate conflict at mid-day on October 18th. The 4th Brigade, under General Westmacott, advanced from the Chagru Kotal against the front of the ridge, while the 3rd Brigade, under General Kempster, swept round to the south and west. This brigade, however, which had set out from Shinwari two hours before daybreak, had been delayed, and was not yet at close quarters, when the Gurkhas, covered by the fire of the Scottish Highlanders from the low ridge opposite the Heights, and by the mountain-gun batteries from Chagru, sprang forward across the open space, and began to climb like mountain cats up the steep and narrow zigzag of the ridge. After them came the Borderers, and the enemy, observing the rapid approach of the stormers, fled before our infantry had reached the summit.

Orders had been given that as soon as the ridge was cleared our men were to return to Shinwari, but their obedience to this order had an unfortunate result. The enemy immediately took it as a sign of weakness, and returned to the attack. They quickly regained the ridge, and, rushing down its front, harassed our retreating men. Thus a brilliant victory assumed the complexion of a defeat, and the moral effect of this upon the tribesmen was not to our advantage.

A more conclusive battle, however, took place two days later at about the same spot. General Lockhart gave orders that the frontal attack on the heights should be combined with an advance down the defile, but in the event General Yeatman-Biggs decided to confine himself to the former. Again the Gurkhas were flung forward. But this time the tribesmen had increased their force, and the brave little men left many dead and wounded in their track. The Dorsetshires and the Sherwood Foresters followed them, and they in their turn suffered very heavily. For a whole hour death was as common as life, but there was no thought of retreat; it was a time for indomitable courage and tenacity.

A moment arrived, about noon, when the 1st Gordons and the 3rd Sikhs prepared for a furious charge. The shrill pipes struck up as the Gordons, led by Colonel Mathias, dashed out into the open space, crossed it, and began to scale the steep hillside beyond. Difficult as this stupendous task appeared to the onlookers, it was achieved by these heroic mountaineers, though not without great loss. Once on the ridge the battle was won. The enemy, unable to check this determined assault, abandoned his position and fled in confusion. This time the ridge was not only cleared, but held for good; and our forces found their way open before them through the Chagru Kotal Pass.

In this Tirah Expedition there was much valuable native blood shed, expecially in the Khurmauna Defile, where a native officer and thirty-five Sikhs were cut off in a ravine and every one of them killed. The Gurkhas, to whom the life of a victory is that only a few come back, had their full share of the joy of battle, with well-earned glory, in this immortal storming of the Dargai Heights.

A LIST OF INDIAN NATIVE REGIMENTS

The following is a list of the Indian Native Regiments from the ranks of which the 70,000 now fighting at the front are drawn:—

Indian Cavalry

Governor-General's Body-Guard.

Battle Honours.—"Java," "Ava," "Maharajpore," "Moodkee," "Ferozeshah," "Aliwal," "Sobraon," "Seetabuldee."

Uniform.—*Scarlet,* facings *blue.*

1st Duke of York's Own Lancers.

(Skinner's Horse.)

Battle Honours.—"Bhurtpore," "Kandahar 1842," "Afghanistan 1879/80," "Pekin 1900."

Uniform.—*Yellow,* facings *black velvet.*

Colonel-in-Chief—THE KING.

2nd Lancers. (Gardner's Horse.)

Battle Honours.—"Arracan," "Sobraon," "Punjab," "Egypt 1882," "Tel-el-Kebir."

Uniform.—*Blue,* facings *light blue.*

A List of Indian Native Regiments

3rd Skinner's Horse.

Battle Honours.—"Afghanistan," "Ghuznee 1839," "Maharajpore," "Khelat," "Moodkee," "Ferozeshah," "Aliwal," "Kandahar 1880," "Afghanistan 1879/80," "Punjab Frontier."

Uniform.—*Blue*, facings *yellow*.

4th Cavalry.

Battle Honour.—"Afghanistan 1879/80."

Uniform.—*Scarlet*, facings *blue*.

5th Cavalry.

Battle Honours.—"Punjab," "Mooltan," "Afghanistan 1879/80."

Uniform.—*Scarlet*, facings *blue*.

6th King Edward's Own Cavalry.

Badges.—The Plume of the Prince of Wales and the Royal and Imperial Cypher of King Edward VII.

Battle Honours.—"Punniar," "Moodkee," "Ferozeshah," "Sobraon," "Egypt 1882," "Tel-el-Kebir," "Punjab Frontier."

Uniform.—*Blue*, facings *scarlet*.

Colonel-in-Chief—THE KING.

7th Hariana Lancers.

Battle Honours.—" Punjab," " Burma 1885/87."

Uniform.—*Scarlet,* facings *blue.*

8th Cavalry.

Battle Honour.—" Afghanistan 1878/80."

Uniform.—*Blue,* facings *scarlet.*

9th Hodson's Horse.

Battle Honours.—" Delhi," " Lucknow," " Suakin 1885," " Chitral," " Punjab Frontier."

Uniform.—*Blue,* facings *white.*

10th Duke of Cambridge's Own Lancers. (Hodson's Horse.)

Battle Honours.—" Delhi," " Lucknow," " Abys sinia," " Afghanistan 1878/80."

Uniform.—*Blue,* facings *scarlet.*

11th King Edward's Own Lancers.

(Probyn's Horse.)

Badges.—The Plume of the Prince of Wales and the Royal and Imperial Cypher of King Edward VII.

Battle Honours.—" Lucknow," " Taku Forts," " Pekin," " Ali Masjid," " Afghanistan 1878/79," " Chitral," " Punjab Frontier," " Malakand."

Uniform.—*Blue,* facings *scarlet.*

Colonel-in-Chief—The King.

A List of Indian Native Regiments

12th Cavalry.

Battle Honours.—"Abyssinia," "Peiwar Kotal," "Charasiah," "Kabul 1879," "Afghanistan 1878/80."

Uniform.—*Blue*, facings *blue*.

13th Duke of Connaught's Lancers.

(Watson's Horse.)

Battle Honours.—"Afghanistan 1878/80," "Egypt 1882," "Tel-el-Kebir," "Punjab Frontier."

Uniform.—*Blue*, facings *scarlet*, lace *silver*.

14th Murray's Jat Lancers.

Battle Honours.—"Charasiah," "Kabul 1879," "Afghanistan 1878/80."

Uniform.—*Blue*, facings *scarlet*, pugri *scarlet*.

15th Lancers. (Cureton's Multanis.)

Battle Honour.—"Afghanistan 1878/80."

Uniform.—*Blue*, facings *scarlet*.

16th Cavalry.

Battle Honour.—"China 1900."

Uniform.—*Blue*, facings *blue*.

17th Cavalry.

Battle Honour.—" Afghanistan 1879/80."

Uniform.—*Blue*, facings *white*.

18th King George's Own Lancers.

Badges.—The Plume of the Prince of Wales and the Royal and Imperial Cypher.

Battle Honours.—" Afghanistan 1879/80," " Punjab Frontier," " Tirah."

Uniform.—*Scarlet*, facings *white*.

19th Lancers. (Fane's Horse.)

Battle Honours.—" Taku Forts," " Pekin," " Ahmad Khel," " Afghanistan 1878/80."

Uniform.—*Blue*, facings *French grey* lace *silver*.

20th Deccan Horse.

Battle Honour.—" Central India."

Uniform.—*Rifle-green*, facings *white*.

21st Prince Albert Victor's Own Cavalry. (Frontier Force.) (Daly's Horse.)

Battle Honours.—" Delhi," " Lucknow," " Ahmad Khel," " Afghanistan 1878/80."

Uniform.—*Blue*, facings *scarlet*.

22nd Sam Browne's Cavalry. (Frontier Force.)

Battle Honours.—" Delhi," " Lucknow," " Ahmad Khel," " Afghanistan 1878/80."

Uniform—*Scarlet*, facings *blue*.

23rd Cavalry. (Frontier Force.)

Battle Honours.—" Kandahar 1880," " Afghanistan 1879/80."

Uniform.—*Blue*, facings *scarlet*.

25th Cavalry. (Frontier Force,)

Battle Honours.—" Delhi," " Lucknow," " Charasiah," " Kabul 1879," " Afghanistan 1878/80."

Uniform.—*Dark green*, facings *scarlet*, pugri *scarlet*.

26th King George's Own Light Cavalry.

Badges.—The Plume of the Prince of Wales and the Royal and Imperial Cypher.

Battle Honours.—" Mysore," " Seringapatam," " Ava," " Afghanistan 1879/80," " Burma 1885/87."

Uniform.—*French grey*, facings *buff*, lace *silver*.

27th Light Cavalry.

Battle Honours.—"Carnatic," "Sholinghur," "Mysore," "Seringapatam," "Burma 1885/87."

Uniform.—*French grey*, facings *buff*, lace *silver*.

28th Light Cavalry.

Battle Honours.—"Mysore," "Seringapatam," "Maheidpoor."

Uniform.—*French grey*, facings *buff*, lace *silver*.

29th Lancers. (Deccan Horse.)

Uniform.—*Rifle green*, facings *white*.

30th Lancers. (Gordon's Horse.)

Battle Honour.—"Central India."

Uniform.—*Rifle green*, facings *white*.

31st Duke of Connaught's Own Lancers.

Battle Honours.—"Afghanistan," "Ghuznee 1839," "Punjab," "Mooltan," "Central India," "Burma 1885/87."

Uniform.—*Blue*, facings *scarlet*.

32nd Lancers.

Battle Honours.—"Central India," "Afghanistan 1879/80."

Uniform.—*Blue*, facings *white*.

33rd Queen Victoria's Own Light Cavalry.

Badge.—The Royal and Imperial Cypher of Queen Victoria within the Garter.

Battle Honours.—"Ghuznee 1842," "Kabul 1842," "Hyderabad," "Persia," "Reshire," "Bushire," "Koosh-ab," "Central India," "Abyssinia," "Kandahar 1880," "Afghanistan 1879/80," "China 1900."

Uniform.—*Blue,* facings *scarlet.*

34th Prince Albert Victor's Own Poona Horse.

Battle Honours.—"Corygaum," "Ghuznee 1839," "Afghanistan," "Kandahar 1842," "Meeanee," "Hyderabad," "Persia," "Reshire," "Koosh-ab," "Bushire," "Kandahar 1880," "Afghanistan 1879/80."

Uniform.—*Blue,* facings *French grey.*

35th Scinde Horse.

Battle Honours.—"Cutchee," "Meeanee," "Hyderabad," "Punjab," "Mooltan," "Goojerat," "Persia," "Central India," "Afghanistan 1878/79."

Uniform.—*Blue,* facings *white,*

36th Jacob's Horse.

Battle Honours.—"Cutchee," "Meeanee," "Hyderabad," "Punjab," "Mooltan," "Goojerat," "Afghanistan 1879/80."

Uniform.—*Blue,* facings *primrose.*

37th Lancers. (Baluch Horse.)

Uniform.—*Khaki serge,* facings *buff.*

38th King George's Own Central India Horse.

Badges.—The Plume of the Prince of Wales and the Royal and Imperial Cypher.

Battle Honours.—"Kandahar 1880," "Afghanistan 1879/80," "Punjab Frontier."

Uniform.—*Drab,* facings *maroon.*

39th King George's Own Central India Horse.

Badges.—The Plume of the Prince of Wales and the Royal and Imperial Cypher.

Battle Honours.—"Kandahar 1880," "Afghanistan 1879/80," "Punjab Frontier."

Uniform.—*Drab,* facings *maroon.*

Colonel-in-Chief—THE KING.

A List of Indian Native Regiments

Cavalry and Infantry

Queen Victoria's Own Corps of Guides

(Frontier Force—Lumsden's).

Badge.—The Cypher of Queen Victoria within the Garter.

Battle Honours.—"Punjab," "Mooltan," "Goojerat," "Delhi," "Ali Masjid," "Kabul 1879," "Afghanistan 1878/80," "Chitral," "Punjab Frontier," "Malakand."

Uniform.—*Drab*, facings *red velvet, scarlet* (cloth) for the ranks.

19th Punjabis. Raised 1857.

4 companies Sikhs, 2 companies Punjabi Mussalmans, 2 companies Pathans.

Battle Honours.—"Ahmad Khel," "Afghanistan '78/80."

Uniform.—*Scarlet*, facings *blue*.

20th Duke of Cambridge's Own Infantry ("Brownlow's Punjabis").

4 companies Pathans, 2 companies Sikhs, 2 companies Dogras.

Battle Honours.—"Taku Forts," "Pekin," "Ali Masjid," "Afghanistan '78/80," "Egypt '82," "Tel-el-Kebir," "Punjab Frontier," "China."

Uniform.—*Drab*, facings *emerald green*.

21st Punjabis. Raised 1857.

3 companies Pathans, 1 company Punjabi Mussalmans, 3 companies Sikhs, 1 company Dogras.

Battle Honours.—"Abyssinia," "Afghanistan '78/80."

Uniform.—*Drab*, facings *scarlet*.

22nd Punjabis. Raised 1857

4 companies Sikhs, 3 companies Punjabi Mussalmans, 1 company Pathans.

Battle Honours.—"China '60/62," "Afghanistan '79/80," "Punjab Frontier."

Uniform.—*Scarlet*, facings *blue*.

23rd Sikh Pioneers. Raised 1857.

8 companies Mazhbi Sikhs.

Battle Honours.—"Taku Forts," "Pekin," "Peiwar Kotal," "Charasiah," "Kabul '79," "Kandahar '80," "Afghanistan '78/80," "Chitral."

Uniform.—*Drab*, facings *chocolate*.

24th Punjabis. Raised 1857.

4 companies Sikhs, 1 company Dogras, 1 company Punjabi Mussalmans, 2 companies Afridis.

Battle Honours.—"Kandahar '80," "Afghanistan '78/80," "Punjab Frontier," "Malakand," "Pekin 1900."

Uniform.—*Scarlet*, facings *white*.

A List of Indian Native Regiments

25th Punjabis. Raised 1857.

3 companies Sikhs, 2 companies Dogras, 2 companies Punjabi Mussalmans, 1 company Pathans.

Battle Honours.—"Ahmad Khel," "Kandahar '80," "Afghanistan '78/80," "Chitral."

Uniform.—*Scarlet*, facings *white*.

26th Punjabis. Raised 1857.

4 companies Sikhs, 2 companies Afridis 2 companies Mussalmans.

Battle Honours.—"Afghanistan '78/80," "Burma '85/87."

Uniform.—*Drab*, facings *scarlet*.

27th Punjabis. Raised 1857.

3 companies Sikhs, 1 company Dogras, 2 companies Punjabi Mussalmans, 2 companies Pathans.

Battle Honours.—"China '60/62," "Ali Masjid," "Afghanistan '78/80," "Burma '85/87."

Uniform.—*Drab*, facings *scarlet*.

28th Punjabis. Raised 1857.

3 companies Sikhs, 1 company Dogras, 3 companies Pathans, 1 company Punjabi Mussalmans.

Battle Honours.—"Charasiah," "Kabul '79," "Afghanistan '78/80."

Uniform.—*Scarlet*, facings *emerald green*.

29th Punjabis. Raised 1857.

4 companies Sikhs, 2 companies Dogras, 2 companies Punjabi Mussalmans.

Battle Honours.—" Peiwar Kotal," " Afghanistan '78/80," " Chitral."

Uniform.—*Scarlet*, facings *blue*.

30th Punjabis. Raised 1857.

4 companies Sikhs, 2 companies Dogras, 2 companies Punjabi Mussalmans.

Battle Honours.—" Afghanistan '79/80," " Chitral," " Punjab Frontier," " Tirah."

Uniform.—*Scarlet*, facings *white*.

31st Punjabis. Raised 1857.

4 companies Sikhs, 2 companies Dogras, 2 companies Punjabi Mussalmans.

Battle Honours.—"Afghanistan '78/80," " Punjab Frontier," " Malakand."

Uniform.—*Scarlet*, facings *white*.

32nd Sikh Pioneers. Raised 1857.

8 companies Mazhbi Sikhs.

Battle Honours.—" Delhi," " Lucknow," " Afgha nistan '78/80," " Chitral."

Uniform.—*Scarlet*, facings *white*.

A List of Indian Native Regiments

33rd Punjabis. Raised 1857.

4 companies Punjabi Mussalmans, 2 companies Pathans, 2 companies Sikhs.

Battle Honour.—"Burma '85/87."

Uniform.—*Drab*, facings *emerald green*.

34th Sikh Pioneers. Raised 1858, disbanded 1887, but recently re-formed.

8 companies Mazhbi Sikhs.

Battle Honours.—"Chitral," "Punjab Frontier," "China 1900."

Uniform.—*Scarlet*, facings *blue*.

35th Sikhs. Raised 1798, disbanded 1882, re-formed 1887.

8 companies Sikhs.

Battle Honours.—"Punjab Frontier," "Malakand."

Uniform.—*Scarlet*, facings *yellow*.

36th Sikhs. Raised 1858, disbanded 1882, re-formed 1887.

8 companies Sikhs.

Battle Honours.—"Punjab Frontier," "Samana," "Tirah."

Uniform.—*Scarlet*, facings *yellow*.

45th Rattray's Sikhs. Raised 1856, added to Bengal Army 1864.

8 companies Sikhs.

Battle Honours.—"Defence of Arrah," "Behar," "Ali Masjid," "Afghanistan '78/80," "Punjab Frontier," "Malakand."

Uniform.—*Scarlet*, facings *white*.

46th Punjabis. Raised 1900.

4 companies Punjabi Mussalmans, 1 company Afridis, 1 company Orakzais, 2 companies Lobana Sikhs.

Uniform.—*Drab*, facings *emerald green*.

47th Sikhs. Raised 1901.

8 companies Sikhs.

Uniform.—*Scarlet*, facings *yellow*.

48th Pioneers. Raised 1901.

4 companies Lobana Sikhs, 4 companies Jats.

Uniform.—*Scarlet*, facings *black*.

51st Sikhs (Frontier Force). Raised 1846.

4 companies Sikhs, 2 companies Punjabi Mussalmans.

Battle Honours.—"Punjab," "Ali Masjid," "Afghanistan '78/79," "Pekin 1900."

Uniform.—*Drab*, facings *yellow*.

52nd Sikhs (Frontier Force). Raised 1846.

3 companies Dogras, 2 companies Sikhs, 2 companies Punjabi Mussalmans, 1 company Pathans.

Battle Honours.—"Punjab," "Ahmad Khel," "Kandahar '80," "Afghanistan '78/80."

Uniform.—*Drab*, facings *scarlet*.

53rd Sikhs (Frontier Force). Raised 1847.

4 companies Sikhs, 1 company Dogras, 2 companies Khattaks, 1 company Punjabi Mussalmans.

Battle Honours.—"Kabul '79," "Kandahar '80," "Afghanistan '79/80," "Punjab Frontier," "Tirah."

Uniform.—*Drab*, facings *black*.

54th Sikhs (Frontier Force). Raised 1847.

4 companies Sikhs, 1 company Dogras, 2 companies Punjabi Mussalmans, 1 company Pathans.

Battle Honours.—"Pegu," "Delhi," "Chitral."

Uniform.—*Drab*, facings *emerald green*.

56th Punjabi Rifles (Frontier Force). Raised 1849.

3 companies Sikhs, 1 company Dogras, 2 companies Punjabi Mussalmans, 2 companies Khattaks.

Battle Honours.—"Delhi," "Lucknow," "Peiwar Kotal," "Afghanistan '78/79," "Punjab Frontier," "Tirah."

Uniform.—*Drab*, facings *black.*

62nd Punjabis. Raised at Madras 1759.

4 companies Punjabi Mussalmans, 2 companies Sikhs, 2 companies Rajputs.

Battle Honours.—"Carnatic," "Mysore," "Assaye," "Nagpore," "China."

Uniform.—*Scarlet*, facings *emerald green.*

66th Punjabis. Raised at Trichinopoly 1761.

4 companies Punjabi Mussalmans, 2 companies Sikhs, 2 companies Rajputs.

Battle Honours.—"Carnatic," "Sholinghur," "Mysore," "Seringapatam," "Bourbon," "China."

Uniform.—*Scarlet*, facings *emerald green.*

A List of Indian Native Regiments

67th Punjabis. Raised at Trichinopoly 1761.

4 companies Punjabi Mussalmans, 2 companies Sikhs, 2 companies Punjabi Hindus.

Battle Honours.—"Carnatic," "Mysore," "Ava."

Uniform.—*Scarlet*, facings *emerald green*.

69th Punjabis. Raised at Madras 1765.

4 companies Punjabi Mussalmans, 2 companies Sikhs, 2 companies Punjabi Hindus.

Battle Honours.—"Carnatic," "Sholinghur," "Mysore," "Ava," "Pegu."

Uniform.—*Scarlet*, facings *emerald green*.

72nd Punjabis. Raised at Cuddalose 1767.

4 companies Sikhs, 2 companies Punjabi Mussalmans, 2 companies Pathans.

Battle Honours.—"Carnatic," "Sholinghur," "Ava," "Burma '85/87."

Uniform.—*Drab serge*, facings *white*.

74th Punjabis. Raised at Vallose 1776.

4 companies Punjabi Mussalmans, 2 companies Sikhs, 2 companies Punjabi Hindus.

Battle Honours.—"Carnatic," "Sholinghur," "Mysore," "Maheidpoor," "China," "Burma '85/87."

Uniform.—*Scarlet*, facings *emerald green*.

Fights of Indian Native Regiments

76th Punjabis. Raised at Trichinopoly 1776.

4 companies Punjabi Mussalmans, 2 companies Sikhs, 2 companies Hindu Jats.

Battle Honours.—" Carnatic," " Sholinghur," " Mysore," " Seringapatam," " Ava," " Burma '85/87."

Uniform.—*Scarlet*, facings *emerald green.*

82nd Punjabis. Raised at Ellore 1788.

2 companies Punjabi Mussalmans, 2 companies Jat Sikhs, 2 companies Hindu Jats.

Battle Honours.—" Mysore," " Seringapatam," " Ava."

Uniform.—*Scarlet*, facings *emerald green.*

84th Punjabis. Raised at Vellore 1794.

4 companies Punjabi Mussalmans, 2 companies Jat Sikhs, 2 companies Rajputs.

Battle Honours.—" Seringapatam," " Assaye," " Bourbon."

Uniform.—*Scarlet*, facings *emerald green.*

87th Punjabis. Raised at Trichinopoly 1798.

4 companies Punjabi Mussalmans, 2 companies Jat Sikhs, 2 companies Hindu Jats.

Battle Honours.—"Maheidpoor," "Lucknow," "Burma '85/87."

Uniform.—*Scarlet*, facings *emerald green*.

89th Punjabis. Raised at Masulipatam 1798.

3 companies Sikhs, 3 companies Punjabi Mussalmans, 1 company Brahmans, 1 company Rajputs.

Uniform.—*Drab serge*, facings *blue*.

90th Punjabis. Raised at Masulipatam 1799.

4 companies Sikhs, 2 companies Punjabi Mussalmans, 1 company Brahmans, 1 company Rajputs.

Battle Honours.—"Ava," "Afghanistan '78/80," "Burma '85/87."

Uniform.—*Drab serge*, facings *black*.

91st Punjabis (Light Infantry). Raised at Trichinopoly 1800.

3 companies Punjabi Mussalmans, 2 companies Sikhs, 2 companies Dogras, 1 company Hindustani Mussalmans.

Battle Honours.—"Maheidpoor," "China 1900."

Uniform.—*Drab*, facings *cherry*.

92nd Punjabis. Raised at Madras 1800.

4 companies Sikhs, 4 companies Punjabi Mussalmans.

Battle Honour.—" Ava."

Uniform.—*Drab serge*, facings *white*.

[For the Gurkha Regiments and others not mentioned in this list the reader is referred to earlier chapters.]

Printed in Great Britain by Hazell, Watson & Viney, Ld., London and Aylesbury—1414681